THE

5 IN 10

PASTA AND
NOODLE
COOKBOOK

Look for these other titles in the *5 in 10* series

The 5 in 10 Cookbook
Paula Hamilton

The 5 in 10 Chicken Breast Cookbook
Melanie Barnard and Brooke Dojny

The 5 in 10 Dessert Cookbook
Natalie Haughton

The 5 in 10 Appetizer Cookbook
Paula Hamilton

THE
5 IN 10
PASTA AND
NOODLE
COOKBOOK

5 Ingredients in
10 Minutes or Less

NANCIE MCDERMOTT

A JOHN BOSWELL ASSOCIATES / KING HILL PRODUCTIONS BOOK

HEARST BOOKS

NEW YORK

To the memory of Selden R. M. Cundiff,
who cooked quick, simple feasts in the kitchen and
took his time at the table with family and friends.

Copyright © 1994 by John Boswell Management, Inc.

It is the policy of William Morrow and Company, Inc., and its imprints and affiliates, recognizing the importance of preserving what has been written, to print the books we publish on acid-free paper, and we exert our best efforts to that end.

Library of Congress Cataloging-in-Publication Data

McDermott, Nancie.
    The 5 in 10 pasta and noodle cookbook : 5 ingredients in 10 minutes
or less / [Nancie McDermott].
        p. cm.
    "A John Boswell Associates/King Hill Productions book."
    Includes index.
    ISBN 0-688-13475-0
    1. Cookery (Pasta). 2. Cookery, International. 3. Quick and easy
cookery. I. Title. II. Title: Five in ten pasta and noodle cookbook.
TX809.M17M375 1994
641.8'22—dc20   94-8504
                                                                 CIP

Printed in the United States of America

First Edition

1 2 3 4 5 6 7 8 9 10

Book design by Barbara Cohen Aronica

CONTENTS

7. SIDE DISH PASTAS 146

Choose a recipe like Orzo with Pesto and Peas, Ziti with Zucchini and Romano Cheese, Peanut Shells, Curry-Curry Couscous, or Tubetti Tabbouleh to round out or dress up the simplest simple meal in a flash.

8. LIGHT AND LEAN PASTAS 158

When you are cutting back on fat, check out these simple ways to eat lean and delicious: Linguine with Tomato-Artichoke Sauce, Warm Pasta Salad with Tomatoes, Grilled Zucchini and Roasted Peppers, Turkey and Spinach Macaroni Bake, Far East Fettuccine and Low-Fat Tuna and Bean Salad.

INDEX 175

INTRODUCTION

Pasta and noodles are foods that everyone, everywhere seems to love. Most of us first came to know their pleasures as children, when we decorated ourselves and our high chair trays with messy nests of spaghetti and dipped into comforting bowls of macaroni and cheese. As we grew older and wiser, we learned to get more pasta in us and less on us and discovered the amazing variety of shapes and flavors possible in this practical, primal food. Nutrition research tells us that pasta is good for us as well as just plain good, adding another reason to put pasta on the menu often. Centering our day-to-day eating on pasta and other complex carbohydrates, such as beans and whole grains, puts us on the pathway to good health.

Cooking pasta is so simple that if you can boil water you're halfway there, and the variety of ways to sauce it and present it are literally too many to count. The recipes I've developed here were inspired by dishes taken from all around the world. For those of us who enjoy both eating and cooking but often find ourselves short on time to spend in the kitchen, pasta is a very good friend, indeed.

This book celebrates pasta and noodle dishes that contain only 5 ingredients, in addition to salt and pepper, and take only 10 minutes to cook. Most dried pastas and all fresh pastas cook within this time limit, dried corkscrew shapes, rigatoni and lasagne noodles being the major exceptions. Except in the soups chapter, your first step will be to bring a large pot of water to a rolling boil. Since this takes a little additional time, do it first thing, before you begin to prep or cook.

To cook pasta quickly and correctly, you need a large pot with a tight-fitting cover, one that will hold at least 4 quarts of water. Add 1 to 2 tablespoons of salt to the water once it boils, and let it return to a rolling boil before adding the pasta. Stir once or twice at the beginning of cooking to separate the noodles and help them cook evenly. Place a colander in the sink when you first put the water on to boil, so you'll be ready to drain the noodles as soon as they're what Italians call *al dente,* tender but still firm "to the tooth," or to the bite. Consider investing in a pot with a colander insert, as this makes it possible to extract and drain the cooked pasta instantly, without hauling the heavy pot of boiling water over to the sink for draining. Drain the pasta well, but not completely, as a little water clinging to the noodles helps prevent sticking and is sometimes part of the sauce. To avoid time-consuming trips to the store when you want dinner in minutes, stock your kitchen with the building blocks for a cornucopia of pastas. Quality counts double when ingredients are few, so splurge on foods that pay you back with their gifts of flavor as well as time. Line your pantry shelf with extra virgin olive oil, sun-dried tomatoes packed in oil, pine nuts, capers, sliced ripe olives, canned clams, tuna, crabmeat, salmon, anchovies and sardines. And don't forget the array of brightly flavored canned tomatoes now on the market, many with herbs and garlic, designed expressly for quick pasta sauces. Keep fresh tomatoes out on the counter in a basket with garlic and onions, so you'll use them often and enjoy their best flavor.

Since freshly grated Parmesan cheese crowns pasta so often, treat yourself to the treasure of imported Parmigiano-Reggiano, still made in the Northern Italian countryside by artisan cheesemakers using traditional methods that are eight centuries old. Aged at least eighteen months, the cheese's extraordinary flavor is best when you store it in two layers of plastic wrap and grate it just before use, since exposure to air dilutes its incomparable aroma and taste. Second choice is to grate it in advance when you have the time and store it in the refrigerator in a plastic storage bag, pressing out all the air before sealing it up. If cost and time are problems, look for freshly grated Parmesan and Pecorino Romano cheese in resealable plastic containers in the cheese section of your supermarket.

This book aims to help you streamline your cooking in starters, soups, salads, side dishes and hearty main courses. Here's hoping these recipes will be like good friends in the kitchen, sharing the work with you and making it more fun the *5 in 10* way.

1 PASTA SNACKS AND STARTERS

Why wait for the main-course pleasures of pasta and noodles when they can be enjoyed as the kickoff to special meals or as a tasty treat in between? Pasta works on antipasti platters and hors d'oeuvre trays, as a stylish first course or a comforting midnight snack.

These recipes offer a little world tour with good-natured mixings of traditional flavors and techniques. When you crave faraway flavors, try Italian Nachos, Gnocchi with Curry Cream Sauce or Spicy Asian Noodles. Come back home with Bow Ties and Buffalo Chicken or Southwestern Spring Rolls. Choose a snack-and-starter pasta to suit your menu and entertaining style. For easy eating, try finger foods such as Couscous-Stuffed Mushrooms, Tortelloni-Artichoke Skewers and Won Ton Sausage Cups. To set an elegant tone for sit-down dinners, offer Capellini with Olivada or Ravioli with Lemon Cream Sauce.

Fresh and frozen wrappers and dumplings play a starring role here in helping make delectable snacks and starters in record time. Check your supermarket refrigerator cases for eggroll and won ton wrappers and fresh tortelloni and tortellini. Ravioli come fresh and frozen, while gnocchi, petite unfilled dumplings made of potato and flour, are usually found frozen in Italian markets. Asian grocery stores offer frozen gyoza or potstickers, oblong meat dumplings that can be boiled, steamed or fried.

COUSCOUS-STUFFED MUSHROOMS

Many people think couscous is a grain, but, in fact, it is a tiny pasta.

$^1/_3$ cup couscous
$^1/_2$ teaspoon salt
16 large (1- to 1$^1/_2$-inch) fresh mushrooms
$^1/_4$ cup pesto sauce
 1 tablespoon finely diced red bell pepper
    Freshly ground pepper
$^1/_3$ cup grated Parmesan cheese

1. Preheat the oven to 400 degrees F. In a small saucepan, bring $^1/_2$ cup water to a boil over high heat. Stir in the couscous and salt, remove from the heat, cover and set aside for at least 5 minutes.

2. Remove the stems from the mushrooms; reserve the stems for another use. Brush the mushroom caps all over with 2 tablespoons of the pesto.

3. Fluff the couscous with a fork and stir in the remaining pesto and the red pepper. Season to taste with pepper and additional salt. Stuff each mushroom cap with 1 heaping tablespoon of couscous. Sprinkle the grated Parmesan cheese on top.

4. Bake the mushrooms for 8 to 10 minutes, until hot.

4 SERVINGS

BOW TIES AND BUFFALO CHICKEN

4 ounces bow tie pasta
1 pound skinless, boneless chicken breast
    Salt and freshly ground pepper
$1/3$ cup flour
8 tablespoons (1 stick) butter
$1/4$ cup hot red pepper sauce

1. Cook the pasta in a large pot of boiling, salted water until tender but still firm, 8 to 10 minutes. Drain well.

2. Meanwhile, cut the chicken breast into 1-inch cubes. Season with salt and pepper and toss with the flour. Shake off and discard the excess flour.

3. Heat 3 tablespoons of the butter in a large frying pan. Add the chicken and cook over medium-high heat, turning, until crisp and golden, 3 to 4 minutes. Add $1/2$ cup of water to the pan and continue cooking until the water evaporates and the chicken is cooked through, 1 to 2 minutes longer.

4. In a small saucepan, melt the remaining 5 tablespoons of butter over medium heat. Stir in the hot pepper sauce. Do not let this mixture boil.

5. In a large serving bowl, combine the drained pasta and pepper-butter sauce with the chicken. Season with salt and pepper to taste and toss well.

4 SERVINGS

CAPELLINI WITH OLIVADA

Olivada is a classic Italian sauce of coarsely chopped olives, olive oil and herbs. Although delicious with canned black olives, this sauce is elevated in flavor if you use imported Niçoise or other oil-cured black olives. These special olives are readily available in delicatessens, gourmet shops and in many supermarkets.

```
 1 pound fresh capellini
 4 large garlic cloves
 1 can (6 ounces) pitted black olives
1/3 cup extra virgin olive oil
1/4 cup capers, undrained
   Salt and freshly ground pepper
```

1. Cook the pasta in a large pot of boiling, salted water until tender but still firm, about 2 minutes. Drain well.

2. Meanwhile, coarsely chop the garlic. In a food processor, combine the olives, olive oil, chopped garlic and capers with their brine. Chop the mixture coarsely using on-off pulses on the machine. Do not puree too finely. The mixture should have a pleasantly chunky texture, but all the ingredients should be combined.

3. Toss the warm, drained pasta with the sauce, season to taste with salt and pepper and serve.

6 TO 8 SERVINGS

ITALIAN NACHOS

Fried fresh pasta chips are crisp and delicious in this takeoff on Mexican nachos. Coarse or kosher salt is available in most grocery stores and is the best choice for seasoning these chips. The chips can be prepared ahead of time through step 2 and stored airtight for future use.

1 pound fresh lasagne noodles
1 cup pasta or spaghetti sauce
3 cups vegetable oil, for frying
1 teaspoon dried Italian seasoning
   Coarse kosher salt
2 cups shredded mozzarella cheese

1. Cut the lasagne noodles into large triangular "chip" shapes. Pour the pasta sauce into a small nonreactive saucepan and set over low heat to warm while you make the nachos.

2. Heat the oil in a large frying pan over medium-high heat. Fry the pasta chips in batches without crowding until crisp and golden, 2 to 3 minutes. Remove the chips from the oil with a slotted spoon and drain on paper towels. Sprinkle the hot chips with the Italian seasoning and coarse salt to taste.

3. On a large serving platter, layer the chips with the shredded mozzarella cheese. Microwave on High for 1 to 2 minutes, until the cheese is melted and bubbly.

4. Serve the nachos immediately, with the warm pasta sauce for dipping.

4 TO 6 SERVINGS

GYOZA POTSTICKERS WITH GINGERED DIPPING SAUCE

Gyoza potstickers are available in a variety of flavors from chicken and cabbage to Thai vegetable. You can find them frozen in some supermarkets and many specialty and Asian markets. If you cannot find pickled ginger, substitute peeled and minced fresh ginger.

16 gyoza potstickers
2½ tablespoons vegetable oil
¼ cup seasoned rice vinegar
¼ cup soy sauce
1 tablespoon minced pickled ginger

1. In a large frying pan, cook the potstickers in the oil over medium-high heat until they begin to brown on one side.

2. Reduce the heat to medium and add ¼ cup of water to the pan. Cover the pan and steam until the bottoms of the potstickers are brown and they are tender, 6 to 8 minutes.

3. In a small bowl, stir together the rice vinegar, soy sauce and pickled ginger. Serve this dipping sauce with the warm potstickers.

4 SERVINGS

Southwestern Spring Rolls

Chinese spring rolls get a surprising twist with a filling of goat cheese and sun-dried tomatoes.

    8 ounces goat cheese
 1/2 cup (4 ounces) oil-packed sun-dried tomatoes, drained
 1/4 cup chopped cilantro
16 spring roll wrappers
  3 cups vegetable oil, for frying

1. Crumble the goat cheese into a medium bowl. Chop the drained sun-dried tomatoes and blend with the goat cheese and chopped cilantro.

2. Place a spring roll wrapper on a flat surface with one corner facing you. Place 2 rounded tablespoons of goat cheese filling in the center of the wrapper. Fold the bottom corner of the wrapper over the filling. Fold the right and left corners of the wrapper over the filling to form an envelope with the top "flap" still open. Brush the top flap with a little cold water and roll the spring roll up neatly and tightly. Repeat this process with the remaining wrappers and filling.

3. Heat the vegetable oil in a large frying pan over medium-high heat until it reaches 375 degrees F. Fry the spring rolls in batches without crowding until golden brown and crispy, 3 to 4 minutes per batch. Remove the spring rolls from the oil and drain on paper towels. Serve warm.

4 to 6 servings

Spicy Asian Noodles

Chile paste and seasoned rice vinegar give these noodles a spicy, sweet and tangy kick. Both ingredients are readily available in Asian food markets or the international section of most grocery stores.

1 pound soba (buckwheat) noodles or spaghetti
$1/4$ cup soy sauce
$1/4$ cup Asian sesame oil
$1/4$ cup seasoned rice vinegar
2 to 3 tablespoons Chinese chile-garlic paste

1. Cook the pasta in a large pot of boiling, salted water until tender but still firm, 7 to 9 minutes. Drain well.

2. In a small bowl, stir together the soy sauce, sesame oil, rice vinegar and chile paste until well blended.

3. Toss the drained pasta with the sauce. Serve at room temperature.

6 to 8 servings

TORTELLONI SKEWERS
WITH TWO DIPPING SAUCES

You'll need about 32 small bamboo skewers for this dish.

18 ounces fresh tortelloni, half spinach and half white
 2 tablespoons pesto sauce
$1/4$ cup mayonnaise
$1/2$ cup Italian salad dressing
$1/4$ cup minced oil-packed sun-dried tomatoes

1. Cook the tortelloni in a large pot of boiling, salted water until tender but still firm, 7 to 8 minutes. Drain and rinse with cold water. Drain again.

2. Thread green and white tortelloni onto each of about 32 bamboo skewers.

3. Mix the pesto and mayonnaise together in a small serving bowl. In another bowl, mix together the Italian dressing and sun-dried tomatoes. Place the skewered tortelloni on a serving platter and serve with the two dipping sauces.

10 TO 12 SERVINGS

RAVIOLI WITH
LEMON CREAM SAUCE

This is an easy, elegant start to a fancy dinner featuring a plain, grilled salmon fillet or veal chop. The richness of the cream is tempered by the tanginess of the lemon. Spinach ravioli or tortelloni would work equally well with this sauce.

10 ounces fresh ravioli, preferably tomato ravioli
 2 cups heavy cream
 1 lemon
 $\frac{1}{4}$ teaspoon salt
 $\frac{1}{4}$ cup chopped fresh Italian parsley
　Freshly ground black pepper

1. Cook the ravioli in a large pot of boiling, salted water until tender but still slightly firm, 7 to 9 minutes. Drain well.

2. Meanwhile, pour the cream into a large frying pan. Bring the cream to a boil, reduce the heat to medium and simmer.

3. While the cream is simmering, grate the colored zest from the lemon and add to the cream. Squeeze the juice from the lemon into the cream and add the salt. Continue simmering until the sauce is reduced to about 1 cup; this will take 8 to 10 minutes. To speed it up, you can raise the heat to high, but watch carefully to be sure it doesn't boil over.

4. Add the drained ravioli and chopped parsley to the saucepan and toss gently to coat with the lemon-cream sauce. Season generously with freshly ground black pepper.

4 SERVINGS

TORTELLONI-ARTICHOKE SKEWERS

You'll need 16 small bamboo skewers for this appetizer.

9 ounces fresh tortelloni
2 jars (6 ounces each) marinated artichoke hearts
16 cherry tomatoes
$1/4$ cup balsamic vinegar
$1/4$ cup chopped fresh Italian parsley
  Salt and freshly ground pepper

1. Cook the tortelloni in a large pot of boiling, salted water until tender but still firm, 7 to 8 minutes. Drain and rinse with cold water; drain well.

2. In a medium bowl, toss the tortelloni with the artichoke hearts and their marinade, the cherry tomatoes, vinegar and parsley. Season with salt and freshly ground pepper to taste.

3. Slide one tortelloni halfway up a bamboo skewer. Follow with an artichoke heart and then a cherry tomato. Finish the remaining skewers in the same fashion.

4. Arrange the tortelloni skewers on a platter and drizzle the marinade remaining in the bowl over the tortelloni.

4 TO 6 SERVINGS

WON TON SAUSAGE CUPS

16 won ton wrappers
 2 tablespoons olive oil
$^{1}/_{2}$ pound spicy Italian sausage
 3 green onions
 1 cup shredded pepper Jack cheese

1. Preheat the oven to 350 degrees F. Brush the won ton wrappers with a little olive oil and press each one into a mini muffin tin to form a cup.

2. Remove the sausage from its casing. Crumble the sausage into a large frying pan and cook over high heat, stirring often, until no longer pink, 3 to 4 minutes. Remove the sausage from the pan with a slotted spoon and drain on paper towels. Thinly slice the green onions.

3. In a small bowl, toss the sausage and green onions to mix well. Divide among the won ton cups. Sprinkle about 1 tablespoon pepper Jack cheese over each cup.

4. Bake in the preheated oven 5 to 7 minutes, until hot and crispy. Serve warm.

6 TO 8 SERVINGS

SHRIMP-IN-BLANKETS

These tasty bites will give pigs-in-a-blanket a run for their money. To prepare ahead, store rolled shrimp a day or so in the refrigerator or freezer, separated well to prevent the wrappers from sticking, and sealed airtight.

16 large shrimp, shelled and deveined, tails on
    Salt and freshly ground pepper
 2 green onions
16 won ton wrappers
 3 cups vegetable oil, for frying
$1/2$ cup Chinese plum sauce

1. Season the shrimp lightly with salt and freshly ground pepper. Using a large, sharp knife, cut the green onions into thin 1-inch-long slivers.

2. Place a won ton wrapper on a flat work surface with one corner facing you. Place a shrimp diagonally in the middle of the wonton wrapper. Sprinkle a few slivers of green onion over the shrimp and wrap it up in the won ton skin, leaving the tail of the shrimp exposed. Moisten the won ton wrapper with a little water to help it stick as you roll it up. Repeat with the remaining won ton wrappers, shrimp and green onions.

3. In a large frying pan, heat the oil over medium-high heat to 375 degrees F. Fry the won tons in batches without crowding until the shrimp are firm and pink and the won ton wrappers are crisp and golden, 2 to 3 minutes per batch. Serve hot, with plum sauce for dipping.

6 TO 8 SERVINGS

WON TONS GENOVESE

Pesto sauce is available in 7- to 10-ounce containers in the refrigerator section of almost every grocery store. Mixed with cream cheese, it makes a simple and savory filling for these fried won tons.

4 ounces cream cheese, softened
2 tablespoons pesto sauce
16 won ton wrappers
3 cups vegetable oil, for frying
$1/2$ cup tomato salsa

1. In a small bowl, stir the cream cheese and pesto together until smooth..

2. Place 1 teaspoon of pesto filling in the center of each won ton wrapper. Moisten the edges of the wrapper with water and fold the wrapper in half, creating a rectangle with a small lump of filling in the center. Moisten the ends of the rectangle, bring them toward each other and pinch together.

3. Heat the oil in a large frying pan over medium-high heat. Fry the won tons in batches without crowding until crisp and golden, 2 to 3 minutes per batch. Remove them from the oil and drain on paper towels. Serve the won tons hot, with tomato salsa for dipping.

4 SERVINGS

CRAB NOODLES IN LETTUCE CUPS

Dry, wiry bean thread noodles come in small skeins wrapped in cellophane. They are found in Asian grocery stores and in the international section of many supermarkets. Made from mung bean flour, they're also called glass noodles, harusame and cellophane noodles. To eat these, each diner rolls up the crab noodles in a lettuce leaf, much as they would a taco.

2 packets (2 ounces each) bean thread noodles
2 tablespoons Chinese chicken salad dressing or sweet-and-sour salad dressing
$^{1}/_{2}$ teaspoon freshly ground pepper
2 cans (6 ounces each) crabmeat
$^{1}/_{3}$ cup chopped cilantro, plus 16 leaves for garnish
16 leaves of Boston, butter or limestone lettuce

1. Bring a covered medium saucepan of water to a rolling boil over high heat. Uncover and add bean thread noodles. Cook 3 minutes, stirring occasionally with a fork to separate the bundles of noodles. Drain well, rinse and drain again.

2. Place the noodles on a cutting board and shape into a long, thick log. Cut crosswise into 2-inch lengths. In a medium bowl, toss the noodles with the dressing and pepper. Add the crabmeat and chopped cilantro and toss well.

3. Arrange the lettuce leaves on a serving platter and divide the noodles among them. Give each an extra grinding of pepper and garnish with a cilantro leaf.

8 TO 12 SERVINGS

SZECHUAN PEANUT DUMPLINGS

Gourmet lettuce mixtures can be found in many supermarket produce sections, sold loose or packaged in 5-ounce cellophane bags; sometimes they are labeled "mesclun." Tasty and convenient, they offer a gorgeous array of greens, including arugula, radicchio, mâche, red oak leaf and baby lettuces. If you wish, substitute romaine, iceberg or leaf lettuce, shredded crosswise into wide ribbons.

18 frozen gyoza or potsticker dumplings
1/2 cup dry-roasted salted peanuts
1/4 cup bottled Thai-style peanut sauce
1/4 cup Chinese plum sauce
 4 cups loosely packed gourmet lettuce mix

1. Cook the potstickers in a large pot of boiling, salted water until the wrappers are tender but firm and the meat filling is cooked through, 3 to 4 minutes. Drain well.

2. Meanwhile, coarsely chop the peanuts. In a medium bowl, stir together the peanut sauce and plum sauce until well blended. Arrange the lettuce on 6 appetizer plates.

3. Add the cooked dumplings to the sauce bowl and tumble gently to coat each one well with the sauce. Using a slotted spoon, transfer 3 dumplings to each plate, placing them like spokes from the center of a wheel. Drizzle the remaining sauce among the plates. Top each serving with a sprinkling of chopped peanuts.

6 SERVINGS

FAR EAST LETTUCE TACOS

Lettuce cups turn dumplings into finger food. Look for gyoza or potsticker dumplings in the freezer case in Asian grocery stores and some supermarkets. Cook them straight from the freezer to keep their wrappers from sticking together and tearing.

16 frozen gyoza or potsticker dumplings
 3 tablespoons Chinese oyster sauce
 1 teaspoon Asian sesame oil
16 cup-shaped leaves of Boston, Bibb or limestone lettuce
1/3 cup small sprigs of cilantro

1. Cook the dumplings in a large pot of boiling, salted water until the wrappers are tender but firm and the meat filling is cooked through, 3 to 4 minutes. Drain.

2. Meanwhile, combine the oyster sauce and sesame oil in a small bowl and stir well. Arrange the lettuce leaves on a large serving platter. Spoon about 1/2 teaspoon of the sauce into each lettuce cup; use the back of a spoon to spread it around a bit.

3. Place a dumpling in each lettuce cup and top with a sprig of cilantro as garnish.

6 TO 8 SERVINGS

TORTELLONI ANTIPASTI

Tortelloni are the larger cousins of tortellini. Wrapped in green spinach pasta, they look terrific on this crowd-pleasing dish. You can substitute tortellini, using several on each skewer. Look for 6-inch bamboo skewers in gourmet shops and supermarkets and keep a supply on hand for *5 in 10* treats.

 9 ounces fresh tortelloni
 1 large red bell pepper
 1/3 cup bottled Italian or vinaigrette salad dressing
    Salt and freshly ground pepper
24 thin slices of salami, preferably Genoa
24 pitted whole ripe olives

1. Cook the tortelloni in a large pot of boiling, salted water until tender but still firm, 7 to 8 minutes. Drain.

2. Meanwhile, cut the red pepper in half lengthwise and discard the stem and seeds. Cut into 24 squares, 1½ to 2 inches each. In a medium bowl, toss the red peppers with the dressing. Season with salt and pepper to taste.

3. Add the cooked tortelloni to the bowl and toss well to coat with dressing. Assemble skewers, starting with a tortelloni, then a slice of salami folded into quarters, a piece of red pepper (piercing its shiny outer side) and finally, an olive. Push all the ingredients close together and down toward the pointed end, so the olive hides the skewer tip.

6 TO 8 SERVINGS

2 PASTA SOUPS

Homemade soup conjures up visions of bright, cozy kitchens filled with laughter, good company and a devoted cook, standing patiently over the stockpot, tending it for hours on end. Few of us have that luxury these days, but that needn't put soup on the back burner for the *5 in 10* cook. With pasta and noodles starring in their classic comfort-food roles and a strong supporting cast of good-quality canned broths, cooked beans and ripe tomatoes seasoned in a cornucopia of ways, delicious, satisfying homemade soups can join your basic culinary repertoire once again.

To keep time and components short and sweet, flavorful players are key. Smoked chicken, turkey, sausage and bacon impart deep, rich notes in a hurry, while fresh basil, rosemary, oregano, cilantro and Italian parsley create a fragrant chorus of herbs.

The classic choices for soups are dried short pasta shapes, from macaroni and small shells to bow ties and little twists. You'll also find the tiny rice-shaped pasta known as orzo, along with cheese-stuffed tortellini, pointy penne, sliced won ton wrappers and unique Thai rice flake noodles, which roll themselves up into delicate scrolls.

These pasta soups are doubly simple to make, since instead of being boiled separately, the noodles usually cook right in the broth. The presence of pasta makes many of them hearty enough to take center stage on your supper table, and like most soups and stews, they taste even better the next day.

SMOKED HAM, ZUCCHINI AND SHELL SOUP

2 cans (14½ ounces each) chicken broth
1 slice of smoked ham (about 2 ounces)
2 small zucchini
½ cup tiny pasta shells
¼ cup freshly grated Parmesan cheese

1. Bring the chicken broth to a boil over high heat in a covered medium saucepan.

2. Meanwhile, cut the ham into ½-inch cubes. Trim the ends from the zucchini and cut lengthwise into quarters. Cut crosswise into ½-inch cubes.

3. When the chicken broth boils, add the ham, zucchini and pasta shells. Return to a boil, reduce the heat to medium and cook uncovered until the pasta is tender but still firm, 7 to 9 minutes.

4. Ladle the soup into serving bowls and sprinkle with the Parmesan cheese.

4 TO 6 SERVINGS

HOPPIN' JOHN SOUP

Hoppin' John, a hearty mixture of black-eyed peas, country ham, onions and long-grain rice, is a classic of the American South. This quick version transforms the traditional main dish into a soup, starring the rice-shaped pasta known as orzo, or *rosamarina*.

2 cans (14$\frac{1}{2}$ ounces each) chicken broth
5 green onions
2 ounces honey-baked ham
$\frac{1}{2}$ cup orzo
1 can (15 ounces) black-eyed peas
   Freshly ground pepper

1. In a covered medium saucepan, bring the chicken broth to a boil over high heat. Meanwhile, cut the green onions into thin slices. Add the sliced white portion to the saucepan; set aside the sliced green tops. Cut the ham into $\frac{1}{2}$-inch dice.

2. Add the orzo to the boiling chicken broth and reduce the heat to medium-high. Cook until the pasta is tender but still firm, about 7 minutes. Drain the black-eyed peas and add to the saucepan along with the ham. Cook 2 minutes longer. Remove from the heat, stir in the sliced green onion tops and season generously with pepper.

4 TO 6 SERVINGS

ANGEL HAIR SOUP WITH CHICKEN AND PINE NUTS

2 boneless chicken breast halves (about 1/2 pound total)
3 ounces fresh angel hair pasta
2 tablespoons fresh Italian parsley
2 cans (14 1/2 ounces each) chicken broth
2 tablespoons pine nuts

1. Cut the chicken into thin strips, 1/4 inch by 1 inch. Cut the pasta into 1-inch pieces. Mince the parsley and set aside.

2. Bring the chicken broth to a boil in a covered medium saucepan over high heat. Add the chicken and reduce the heat to medium-high. Cook, stirring occasionally, until the chicken is almost cooked through, about 1 minute. Add the angel hair pasta and cook until tender but still firm, 2 minutes longer.

3. Meanwhile, place the pine nuts in a small, dry frying pan over medium heat. Cook, stirring occasionally, until golden brown, about 3 minutes.

4. To serve, spoon the soup into bowls and garnish with the pine nuts and minced parsley.

4 TO 6 SERVINGS

PASTA E FAGIOLI

Tubetti are tiny tubes also known as salad macaroni. Use white navy beans or red kidney beans instead of cannellini beans if you like. This thick soup is a meal in a bowl.

1 can (15 ounces) cannellini beans
1 can (14½ ounces) beef broth
1 can (14 to 16 ounces) Italian-style stewed tomatoes, undrained
1 cup tubetti
Salt and freshly ground pepper
⅓ cup freshly grated Parmesan cheese

1. Drain the cannellini beans into a colander. Rinse well under cold running water and drain again.

2. In a medium saucepan, combine the beans, beef broth and tomatoes. Cover and bring to a rolling boil over high heat.

3. Add the tubetti. Reduce the heat to medium and cook uncovered for about 7 minutes, until the pasta is tender but still firm. Season with salt and pepper to taste. Divide the soup among individual serving bowls and sprinkle each with cheese.

4 TO 6 SERVINGS

PASTA E CECI

Chick-peas are also known as garbanzo beans and in Italy they are called *ceci*. This traditional soup makes a satisfying meal right from the stove, but it's even better in an encore performance, after its flavors have deepened overnight.

1 can (14½ ounces) chicken broth
1 can (14 to 16 ounces) Italian-style stewed tomatoes
2 tablespoons finely chopped fresh rosemary or 1½ teaspoons
   dried
1 can (15½ ounces) chick-peas
1 cup elbow macaroni
   Salt and freshly ground pepper

1. In a medium saucepan, combine the chicken broth, tomatoes and 1 tablespoon of the fresh rosemary or ¾ teaspoon dried. Cover and bring to a rolling boil over high heat. Meanwhile, drain the chick-peas, rinse them and drain again.

2. Add the macaroni to the broth, reduce the heat to medium-high and cook uncovered, stirring often, until the macaroni is tender but still firm, 7 to 8 minutes.

3. Combine 1 cup of the hot broth with ½ cup of the drained chick-peas in a blender or food processor. Puree until smooth, about 30 seconds. Add the chick-pea puree and remaining chick-peas and rosemary to the soup and cook until heated through, about 1 minute. Add salt to taste and season generously with freshly ground pepper.

4 TO 6 SERVINGS

ORZO SOUP WITH SAUSAGE AND SPINACH

1 package (10 ounces) frozen chopped spinach, thawed
1 Italian sausage link ($^1/_4$ pound), preferably hot
2 cans (14$^1/_2$ ounces each) chicken broth
$^1/_4$ cup orzo
$^1/_4$ cup freshly grated Parmesan or Romano cheese

1. Drain the spinach well and squeeze dry, reserving half for another use. Remove the casing from the sausage and crumble the meat.

2. Place the sausage in a medium saucepan. Cook over medium-high heat, stirring occasionally, until it is browned, about 2 minutes. Drain off the fat, if any.

3. Stir in the spinach and chicken broth and bring to a boil. Add the orzo and cook until tender but still firm, about 7 minutes.

4. To serve, spoon the soup into bowls and sprinkle with the cheese.

4 SERVINGS

SAUSAGE AND SWEET PEPPER PASTA SOUP

1 Italian sausage link ($^1/_4$ pound)
$^1/_4$ large red bell pepper
2 cans (14$^1/_2$ ounces each) chicken broth
$^1/_2$ cup multicolor pasta twists
$^1/_4$ cup frozen peas, thawed

1. Remove the casing from the sausage and crumble the meat. Cut the red bell pepper into $^1/_4$-inch dice.

2. Place the sausage and red pepper in a medium saucepan. Cook over medium-high heat until the sausage is browned, about 2 minutes. Drain off all the fat.

3. Add the chicken broth to the saucepan and bring to a boil. Add the pasta twists and cook until tender but still firm, about 8 minutes. Stir in the peas and serve.

4 SERVINGS

MACARONI WITH BACON
IN TOMATO BROTH

2 slices of bacon
4 green onions
1 can (14$\frac{1}{2}$ ounces) chicken broth
1 can (14 ounces) "pasta-ready" tomatoes, undrained
$\frac{1}{2}$ cup elbow macaroni

1. Slice the bacon crosswise into $\frac{1}{2}$-inch pieces. Slice the green onions into $\frac{1}{2}$-inch pieces. Combine the bacon and green onions in a medium saucepan. Cook over medium-high heat until the bacon begins to crisp, 2 to 3 minutes.

2. Add the chicken broth and tomatoes with their juice, cover and bring to a boil over high heat. Add the macaroni and cook uncovered until tender but still firm, 7 to 8 minutes.

4 SERVINGS

TUSCAN BEAN AND PASTA SOUP

1 can (15 ounces) cannellini beans
2 cans (14½ ounces each) chicken broth
½ teaspoon dried rosemary
½ cup spinach or multicolored macaroni
1 cup shredded cooked chicken

1. Drain the cannellini beans into a colander. Rinse well under cold running water; drain well.

2. Place the chicken broth, 1 cup water and the dried rosemary in a medium saucepan. Bring to a boil over medium-high heat. Add the macaroni and cook until tender but still firm, about 8 minutes.

3. Reduce the heat to medium, add the beans and chicken and heat through, about 2 minutes. Serve hot.

4 SERVINGS

KIELBASA AND BOW TIE SOUP

2 tablespoons Italian parsley
$^{1}/_{4}$ pound smoked garlic sausage, such as kielbasa
1 can (14$^{1}/_{2}$ ounces) chicken broth
1 can (15 ounces) "pasta-ready" tomatoes, undrained
1$^{1}/_{2}$ cups bow tie pasta

1. Mince the parsley and set aside. Cut the sausage into $^{1}/_{4}$-inch slices.

2. Place the sausage in a medium saucepan. Cook over medium-high heat, stirring often, until it is lightly browned, 1 to 2 minutes.

3. Add the chicken broth and tomatoes to the sausage, cover and bring to a boil over high heat. Uncover, add the pasta and cook until tender but still firm, 8 to 9 minutes.

4. To serve, spoon the soup into bowls and sprinkle with the parsley.

4 SERVINGS

TORTELLINI SOUP WITH HAM AND ZUCCHINI

4 ounces smoked ham
1 medium zucchini
2 cans (14½ ounces each) chicken broth
¼ pound fresh cheese tortellini

1. Cut the ham into ½-inch dice. Cut the zucchini into ½-inch pieces.

2. Bring the chicken broth and 1½ cups water to a boil in a covered medium saucepan over medium-high heat. Add the tortellini and cook uncovered 4 minutes. Add the ham and zucchini and continue to cook until the pasta is tender but still firm, 2 to 3 minutes longer.

4 SERVINGS

WON TON SOUP

20 won ton wrappers
 4 ounces cooked ham
 2 green onions
 2 cans (14½ ounces each) chicken broth
 2 teaspoons Asian sesame oil

1. Stack the won ton wrappers in 3 piles and cut into ½-inch-wide strips. Cut the ham into ¼-inch dice and chop the green onions.

2. Bring the chicken broth and 1½ cups water to a boil in a covered medium saucepan over high heat. Uncover and reduce the heat to medium.

3. Add the won ton wrappers, ham and green onions. Simmer 3 minutes, or until the won ton strips are tender but still firm. Stir in the sesame oil and serve immediately.

4 SERVINGS

BOW TIE SHRIMP SOUP

2 cans (14½ ounces each) chicken broth
1 cup bow tie pasta
½ pound medium shrimp, shelled and deveined
2 tablespoons fresh lime juice
2 tablespoons chopped cilantro

1. Bring the broth to a boil over medium-high heat in a medium saucepan. Add the pasta and cook 4 minutes.

2. Add the shrimp and cook until the shrimp are pink and curled and the pasta is tender but still firm, about 4 minutes longer.

3. Remove from the heat, stir in the lime juice and chopped cilantro and serve.

4 SERVINGS

MEXICAN FIESTA SOUP

1 can (14½ ounces) chicken or vegetable broth
2 tablespoons cilantro
1 can (15 ounces) black beans
1 can (15 ounces) Mexican-style stewed tomatoes
½ cup elbow macaroni

1. Bring the broth to a boil in a covered medium saucepan over high heat. Meanwhile, finely chop the cilantro and set aside. Drain the beans into a colander and rinse well under cold running water; drain again.

2. Stir the tomatoes and macaroni into the boiling broth. Return to a boil and cook uncovered, stirring occasionally and breaking up the tomatoes with the side of a large spoon, until the pasta is tender but still firm, 7 to 8 minutes.

3. Reduce the heat to medium and stir in the beans and 1 tablespoon of the chopped cilantro. Cook until heated through, 1 to 2 minutes. To serve, ladle into bowls. Sprinkle the remaining cilantro on top.

4 SERVINGS

CURLY THAI RICE NOODLE SOUP

Asian markets usually dedicate an entire aisle to dried noodles; there you'll find rice flakes, a treasure well worth a bit of detective work. Look for 8-ounce cellophane bags filled with flat, translucent, off-white chips. Buy a supply for your pantry, as they keep well and leave us *5 in 10* cooks with minutes to spare.

½ pound dried rice flakes
3 cups salad-ready spinach leaves
2 links (½ pound) hot and spicy Italian sausage
2 cans (14½ ounces each) chicken broth
¼ cup chopped cilantro

1. Bring a large, covered pot of water to a rolling boil over high heat. Meanwhile, tear the spinach into 2-inch pieces. Cut open the sausage casings to expose the ground meat.

2. Add the rice flakes to the boiling water and cook uncovered, stirring often in a clockwise direction, until the noodles turn bright white, roll up into tight little scrolls and are tender but still firm, about 2 minutes; drain well.

3. In a medium saucepan, combine the 2 cans of chicken broth with 1 can of water. Cover and bring to a boil over high heat. Crumble in the sausage meat and boil, stirring occasionally, 3 to 4 minutes, until the sausage is cooked through. Add the spinach and cooked rice flakes, stir well and cook 1 minute longer. Garnish with the cilantro.

4 TO 6 SERVINGS

3 PASTA SALADS

Pasta salads are the popular, newfangled, all-American contribution to the pasta world.

Some of these salads often resemble main dishes, since pasta satisfies the appetite so well. Others, with robust flavors from pesto to sun-dried tomatoes, make terrific side dishes to accompany simple foods, such as grilled chicken, leftover meats or cooked shrimp. Served with steamed vegetables or a crisp green salad, they let you "do lunch" in a jiffy. Since many taste best at room temperature, they shine on a buffet for entertaining or as your contribution to a potluck meal.

Short pastas are the ideal shapes for salads, since they're easy to eat and showcase chunky ingredients in a pleasing jumble. After cooking pasta for salads, it is a good idea to rinse the drained noodles under cold running water to prevent sticking, then drain well. Add a little extra dressing and season generously if you plan to chill the salad and serve later, since the pasta tends to absorb the sauce as it sits. Pasta salads served ice cold lose much of their appeal, as a deep chill dulls their pleasing texture and flavor. Serving them either warm or at room temperature is the ideal way. When holding them for later, cover and chill but try to remove from the refrigerator in time to sit 20 minutes or so at room temperature, or warm them up gently in the microwave, without allowing them to heat up or cook.

SUMMER SUNBURST TOMATO SALAD

Look for brilliantly colored pear-shaped tomatoes in farmers' markets or the specialty produce section. If they're hard to find, use cherry tomatoes and cooked new potatoes.

  9 ounces fresh angel hair pasta
  1 pint small red pear tomatoes
  1 pint small yellow pear tomatoes
  1 cup bottled Italian salad dressing with Parmesan cheese
  1/2 cup shredded fresh basil leaves
    Freshly ground pepper

1. Cook the pasta in a large pot of boiling, salted water until tender but still firm, about 2 minutes. Drain and rinse with cold water; drain well.

2. Slice the red and yellow pear tomatoes in half lengthwise and toss with the dressing in a microwave-safe bowl. Cover the bowl and microwave on High for 30 seconds, until the tomatoes start releasing their juices.

3. Toss the pasta with the tomatoes and dressing and add the basil. Season with freshly ground pepper to taste. Serve at room temperature or lightly chilled.

4 TO 6 SERVINGS

GERMAN PASTA SALAD

Instead of potato salad, tote this quick, hearty dish to your next picnic and watch them smile.

$1/2$ pound ziti
$1/2$ small cabbage
$1/2$ pound cooked ham
 2 medium carrots
$1/3$ cup bottled poppyseed salad dressing
    Salt and freshly ground pepper

1. Cook the pasta in a large pot of boiling, salted water for 7 minutes. Add the cabbage (in 1 piece) and cook until the pasta is tender but still firm and the cabbage is bright green, 2 to 3 minutes longer. Drain and rinse in cold water. Drain well. Cut out the tough core and cut the cabbage into 1-inch pieces.

2. While the pasta is cooking, cut the ham into $1/4$-inch dice. Peel the carrots and shred them in a food processor or on the large holes of a hand grater.

3. In a large bowl, toss the pasta and cabbage with the ham, carrots and poppyseed dressing. Season with salt and pepper to taste and toss well.

4 TO 6 SERVINGS

WILD WEST WAGON WHEELS

You won't need a chuckwagon to toss together this spunky, delicious pasta. If you need to please kids and grown-ups, this is your dish.

$1/2$ pound wagon wheel pasta
$1/2$ pound smoked chicken
 1 can (15 ounces) black beans
 1 cup hot and spicy tomato salsa
$1/3$ cup chopped cilantro
   Salt and freshly ground pepper

1. Cook the pasta in a large pot of boiling, salted water until tender but still firm, 8 to 9 minutes. Drain and rinse in cold water; drain well.

2. While the pasta is cooking, cut the chicken into $1/2$-inch cubes. Drain the beans into a colander. Rinse under cold running water and drain well.

3. In a large bowl, combine the pasta with the chicken, drained black beans, salsa and cilantro and toss well. Season with salt and pepper to taste.

6 TO 8 SERVINGS

SHRIMP CAESAR SALAD

$1/4$ pound bow tie pasta
$1/2$ head of romaine lettuce
$1/2$ pound cooked bay shrimp
$1/2$ cup bottled Caesar salad dressing
 1 cup herbed croutons
   Salt and freshly ground pepper

1. Cook the pasta in a large pot of boiling, salted water until tender, 8 to 9 minutes. Drain and rinse in cold water; drain well.

2. While the pasta is cooking, tear the lettuce into bite-size pieces and place in a salad bowl.

3. Add the shrimp, pasta and dressing to the lettuce and toss. Add the croutons and salt and pepper to taste and toss well.

4 SERVINGS

CHINESE CHICKEN SALAD

$3/4$ pound boneless cooked chicken
1 head of romaine lettuce
4 green onions
1 can (5 ounces) chow mein noodles
1 cup bottled Chinese chicken salad dressing or sesame
  dressing

1. Tear the chicken into shreds. Cut the lettuce into bite-size pieces and place in a salad bowl. Slice the green onions on an angle into 1-inch lengths and add to the lettuce.

2. Add the chicken and chow mein noodles to the salad and just before serving pour in the dressing. Toss and serve immediately.

6 SERVINGS

BACON, TOMATO AND AVOCADO BOW TIES

$^1\!/_2$ pound bow tie pasta
 8 slices of bacon
 1 large firm ripe tomato
 1 large ripe avocado
$^1\!/_2$ cup mayonnaise

1. Cook the pasta in a large pot of boiling, salted water until tender but still firm, 8 to 9 minutes. Drain and rinse in cold water; drain well.

2. While the pasta is cooking, slice the bacon crosswise into 1-inch pieces. Cook the bacon in a large frying pan over medium-high heat, turning occasionally, until crispy, 2 to 3 minutes. Drain on paper towels and set aside.

3. Cut the tomato in half crosswise and gently squeeze out the seeds. Dice the tomato in $^1\!/_2$-inch pieces. Peel the avocado and cut into $^1\!/_2$-inch dice. Gently rinse the avocado in cold water to keep it from turning dark.

4. Gently toss the cooled pasta, bacon, tomato and avocado together in a medium bowl. Add the mayonnaise and fold in gently.

4 TO 6 SERVINGS

BOW TIES WITH ARTICHOKE HEARTS AND SUN-DRIED TOMATOES

1/2 pound bow tie pasta
3 green onions
1 jar (6 ounces) marinated artichoke hearts
1/4 cup oil-packed sun-dried tomatoes, plus 1 1/2 tablespoons of the oil
1 tablespoon fresh lemon juice
Salt and freshly ground pepper

1. Cook the pasta in a large pot of boiling, salted water until tender but still firm, 8 to 9 minutes. Drain, rinse in cold water and drain again. Set aside in a serving bowl.

2. While the pasta is cooking, cut the green onions crosswise into very thin slices. Drain the artichoke hearts, reserving the marinade; cut the artichokes into quarters. Chop the sun-dried tomatoes into 1/2-inch pieces, reserving 1 1/2 tablespoons of the oil from the jar.

3. Whisk together the artichoke marinade, sun-dried tomato oil and fresh lemon juice.

4. In a medium bowl, toss the artichoke hearts, sun-dried tomatoes and green onions with the pasta. Add the dressing and toss well. Season with salt and pepper to taste.

4 TO 6 SERVINGS

CHICKEN AND CHUTNEY PASTA SALAD

$^1/_2$ pound ziti
3 green onions
$^1/_2$ cup mango chutney
$^1/_2$ cup mayonnaise
2 cups shredded cooked chicken
    Salt and freshly ground pepper

1. Cook the pasta in a large pot of boiling, salted water until tender but still firm, 8 to 10 minutes. Drain and rinse in cold water; drain well.

2. While the pasta is cooking, cut the green onions crosswise into very thin slices. Chop the fruit in the chutney.

3. In a medium bowl, stir together the chutney with its chopped fruit and the mayonnaise until well blended. Add the cooled pasta, green onions and chicken and toss until well combined.

4 TO 6 SERVINGS

SMOKED CHICKEN SPINACH SALAD

Salad-ready spinach is a terrific time-saver for the *5 in 10* cook. If you like sharp, pungent flavors, use tender, leafy sprigs of watercress instead.

1/2 pound ziti
1/2 pound smoked chicken
 1 small red onion
 3 cups salad-ready spinach leaves
1/2 cup bottled vinaigrette or Italian dressing
    Salt and freshly ground pepper

1. Cook the pasta in a large pot of boiling, salted water until tender but still firm, 8 to 10 minutes. Drain and rinse in cold water. Drain well.

2. Meanwhile, cut the chicken into 1-inch chunks. Chop the onion.

3. Combine the chicken and the spinach in a large serving bowl and toss. In a large frying pan over medium heat, warm the dressing for about 1 minute. Add the onion and cook 1 minute, stirring often. Add the pasta and toss well.

4. Add the sauced pasta to the serving bowl and toss. Season with salt and freshly ground pepper and toss well.

4 SERVINGS

SAIGONNAIS CRABMEAT NOODLES

This is my *5 in 10* version of a tasty Vietnamese-style rice noodle salad shared with me by my friend Tin Quan, chef/owner of Saigonnais Restaurant in Washington, D.C. These wire-thin dried rice noodles are also called rice sticks, rice vermicelli and *mai-fun*, and are widely available in Asian grocery stores and many supermarkets.

3 ounces thin dried rice noodles
5 large garlic cloves
2 tablespoons extra virgin olive oil
   Salt and freshly ground pepper
1 can (6 ounces) crabmeat, drained
¼ cup chopped cilantro

1. Bring a medium saucepan of water to a rolling boil over high heat. Stir in the noodles and remove from the heat. Use 2 forks to stir and separate the noodles, then let them soak for 5 minutes until softened and bright white. Drain and place on a cutting board in a log-shaped pile. Cut crosswise into 2-inch lengths. You'll have about 2½ cups.

2. Meanwhile, chop the garlic. In a large frying pan over medium heat, combine the oil and garlic and cook, stirring often, about 2 minutes. Increase the heat to medium-high and add the noodles, salt and pepper. Cook, stirring often, 4 to 5 minutes, until the noodles are tender but still firm. Add the crabmeat, cilantro and additional pepper and toss well.

4 SERVINGS

CURRIED SHRIMP SALAD

$1/2$ pound bow tie pasta
 2 teaspoons curry powder
$1/2$ cup Italian or vinaigrette dressing
$1/2$ pound cooked bay shrimp
 2 tablespoons chopped cilantro
    Salt and freshly ground pepper

1. Cook the pasta in a large pot of boiling, salted water until tender but still firm, 8 to 9 minutes. Drain and rinse in cold water; drain well.

2. While the pasta is cooking, combine the curry powder and salad dressing and stir well.

3. In a medium bowl, stir together the pasta, dressing, shrimp and cilantro. Season with salt and pepper and toss well.

4 TO 6 SERVINGS

DILLY SHRIMP SALAD

$1/2$ pound elbow macaroni
 3 tablespoons chopped fresh dill or 1 teaspoon dried
$1/4$ cup mayonnaise
$1/4$ cup sour cream
$1/2$ pound cooked bay shrimp
    Salt and freshly ground pepper

1. Cook the pasta in a large pot of boiling, salted water until tender but still firm, 7 to 8 minutes. Drain and rinse in cold water; drain well.

2. While the pasta is cooking, combine the dill, mayonnaise and sour cream and stir well.

3. In a medium bowl, combine the pasta, shrimp and dressing and toss. Season to taste with salt and pepper and toss well.

4 TO 6 SERVINGS

CURRIED CHICKEN SALAD

$1/2$ pound wagon wheel pasta
2 cups cooked chicken meat
1 cup red seedless grapes
2 teaspoons curry powder
$1/2$ cup mayonnaise
   Salt and freshly ground pepper

1. Cook the pasta in a large pot of boiling, salted water until tender but still firm, 8 to 9 minutes. Drain and rinse with cold water; drain well.

2. While the pasta is cooking, cut up the chicken into 1-inch chunks. Cut the grapes in half lengthwise. Combine the curry powder and mayonnaise and stir well.

3. In a medium bowl, combine the pasta, chicken, grapes and curry dressing and toss. Season to taste with salt and pepper and toss well.

4 SERVINGS

Straw and Hay Tortellini

$1/2$ large red bell pepper
1 small bunch of broccoli
$1/2$ cup prepared oil and vinegar or Italian salad dressing
$1/4$ cup prepared pesto sauce
$1/4$ pound each fresh spinach and egg tortellini

1. Bring a large pot of salted water to a boil over high heat.

2. Meanwhile, cut the red bell pepper into $1/4$-inch dice to make about $1/2$ cup. Cut the broccoli florets into bite-size pieces to make about $1 1/2$ cups. Stir together the dressing with the pesto sauce until well blended.

3. Add the broccoli to the boiling water. Cook until just tender and bright green, about 2 minutes. Remove the broccoli and rinse under cold water. Set aside with the red bell pepper.

4. Add the tortellini to the boiling water and cook until tender, about 7 to 8 minutes. Drain and rinse in cold water. Drain well. Toss the tortellini with the broccoli, red bell pepper and pesto dressing.

4 TO 6 SERVINGS

ITALIAN TORTELLINI SALAD

9 ounces fresh cheese tortellini
1 medium cucumber
1 jar (7½ ounces) roasted red peppers, drained
2 or 3 green onions
½ cup Italian salad dressing

1. Cook the tortellini in a large pot of boiling, salted water until tender, 6 to 7 minutes. Drain and rinse in cold water; drain well.

2. While the pasta is cooking, peel and seed the cucumber and cut into ¼-inch dice. Cut the red peppers into 1-inch squares. Chop enough of the green onions to make ¼ cup.

3. Toss together the cooked tortellini, cucumber, red pepper and green onions. Add the Italian dressing and mix well.

4 SERVINGS

SHELLS WITH TOMATOES AND OLIVES

$^1\!/_2$ pound tiny shell pasta
8 ounces mozzarella cheese
1 can (14 to 16 ounces) Italian-style stewed tomatoes
1 can (14$^1\!/_2$ ounces) sliced black olives, drained
3 tablespoons extra virgin olive oil
   Salt and freshly ground pepper

1. Cook the pasta in a large pot of boiling, salted water until tender, 7 to 8 minutes. Drain and rinse in cold water; drain well.

2. While the pasta is cooking, cut the mozzarella cheese into $^3\!/_8$-inch dice. Drain the tomatoes, reserving $^1\!/_3$ cup of the juice. Chop the tomatoes coarsely. Stir the olive oil into the tomato juice to make the dressing.

3. In a mixing bowl, combine the cold pasta, cheese, tomatoes, sliced olives and dressing. Toss well to combine and season with salt and pepper to taste.

6 TO 8 SERVINGS

SOUTHWESTERN MACARONI SALAD

$1/2$ pound salad or elbow macaroni
$1/4$ cup fresh cilantro
1 jar ($7^{1}/_{2}$ ounces) roasted red peppers
1 can (4 ounces) diced green chiles
$3/4$ cup mayonnaise
    Salt and freshly ground pepper

1. Cook the pasta in a large pot of boiling, salted water until tender, 7 to 9 minutes. Drain and rinse in cold water; drain well.

2. While the pasta is cooking, chop the cilantro and set aside. Cut the roasted peppers into $1/2$-inch pieces. Drain the chiles.

3. In a mixing bowl, combine the cold pasta, cilantro, roasted red peppers, diced chiles and mayonnaise. Toss well. Season to taste with salt and pepper.

6 SERVINGS

PESTO PASTA SALAD

1 pound bow tie pasta
1 jar (7½ ounces) roasted red peppers
1 can (2¼ ounces) sliced black olives, drained
¾ cup prepared pesto sauce
1 to 1½ cups mayonnaise
Salt and freshly ground pepper

1. Cook the pasta in a large pot of boiling, salted water until tender, 8 to 9 minutes. Drain and rinse in cold water; drain well.

2. While the pasta is cooking, cut the roasted red peppers into long, thin strips.

3. In a large mixing bowl, stir together the cold pasta, roasted pepper strips, sliced olives, pesto sauce and mayonnaise. Toss well. Season with salt and pepper to taste.

8 SERVINGS

ZITI WITH TOMATOES AND HERBS

$1/2$ pound ziti
$1/4$ cup fresh basil, dill or cilantro sprigs
 2 medium tomatoes
$1/4$ pound feta cheese
 6 tablespoons extra virgin olive oil
    Salt and freshly ground pepper

1. Cook the pasta in a large pot of boiling, salted water until tender but still firm, 8 to 10 minutes. Drain and rinse in cold water; drain well.

2. While the pasta is cooking, mince the fresh herbs and set aside. Seed the tomatoes and cut into $1/4$-inch dice.

3. Crumble the feta cheese into a medium bowl and add the olive oil. Stir with a fork to mash and mix together well.

4. Add the cold pasta, fresh herbs and tomatoes to the feta and olive oil. Season to taste with salt and pepper. Toss well to mix.

6 SERVINGS

THAI CHICKEN AND PASTA SALAD

$1/2$ pound ziti
$1/2$ pound boneless cooked chicken
$1/4$ cup fresh cilantro sprigs
$1/4$ cup spicy Thai peanut sauce
 2 tablespoons vegetable oil
   Salt and freshly ground pepper

1. Cook the pasta in a large pot of boiling, salted water until tender, 8 to 10 minutes. Drain and rinse until cold; drain well.

2. While the pasta is cooking, tear the chicken into shreds. Mince the cilantro and set aside. In a large bowl, stir together the peanut sauce and oil to make the salad dressing.

3. Add the cold pasta, cilantro and chicken to the peanut dressing and toss well. Season to taste with salt and pepper.

4 SERVINGS

4 PASTA CLASSICS

Here are *5 in 10* versions of some of the greatest hits of the pasta and noodle world, steamlined for when you're short on time and energy. This classics chapter has a heavy Italian accent, celebrating the wealth of delicious, uncomplicated pasta dishes enjoyed for centuries on the everyday tables of Italy.

Some of the simplest pastas already come in under the five-ingredient guideline, including Fettuccine Alfredo, Macaroni and Cheese, and Spaghetti Carbonara. Other dishes, such as Linguine with Clam Sauce, Dan Dan Noodles and Fettuccine alla Romana called for a bit of tinkering to keep time and ingredients on the short-and-sweet side.

Serving sizes in this chapter vary somewhat, because many of these dishes can be presented either as a separate pasta course to begin the meal or as a small main-course portion. As a rule of thumb for these, I've allowed 2 to 3 ounces of fresh pasta and 3 to 4 ounces of dried per person. Others, more appropriate as side dishes, call for smaller amounts. Most dishes that serve 3 to 4 can be doubled to serve more people or to allow for larger portions.

Abundant shortcuts to classic pastas await you in supermarkets and specialty food shops these days. In addition to the variety of tomato sauce jars on the shelf, the refrigerator case is stocked with Alfredo sauce, four-cheese sauce, both basil and sun-dried tomato pesto, and freshly grated Parmesan and Romano cheeses.

FETTUCCINE ALFREDO

Splurge on best-quality Parmesan cheese for this simple, luxurious dish. Balance its richness with a sprightly salad of Boston lettuce and watercress with a red wine vinaigrette dressing.

  9 ounces fresh fettuccine
  2 tablespoons butter
$^1/_2$ cup heavy cream
$^1/_2$ cup freshly grated Parmesan cheese
$^1/_2$ teaspoon freshly grated nutmeg
    Salt and freshly ground pepper

1. Cook the pasta in a large pot of boiling, salted water until tender but still firm, 3 to 4 minutes. Drain well.

2. While the pasta is cooking, combine the butter and cream in a large frying pan over medium heat. Cook 2 minutes, stirring often, until the butter is melted and the cream is bubbly and heated through. Remove from the heat.

3. When the pasta is cooked and drained, add it to the frying pan and toss over low heat, lifting the strands to coat them with the sauce. Add the cheese, nutmeg, salt and pepper and toss well. Continue to toss over low heat until the cheese is mixed in and melted and the sauce thickens and coats the pasta well, 1 to 2 minutes. Serve immediately.

3 TO 4 SERVINGS

SPAGHETTI CON AGLIO E OLIO

The name of this dish means "spaghetti with garlic and olive oil," and while it's especially dear to Roman hearts, versions of it have been served as comfort food all over Italy for centuries. For lovers of the "stinking rose," there's garlic galore. If you're fond of chile heat, add a dash of crushed hot red pepper to the oil along with the garlic.

½ pound spaghetti
5 large garlic cloves
¼ cup extra virgin olive oil
2 tablespoons chopped Italian parsley
   Salt and freshly ground pepper

1. Cook the pasta in a large pot of boiling, salted water until tender but still firm, 8 to 9 minutes. Drain well.

2. Meanwhile, chop the garlic. Combine the olive oil and garlic in a large frying pan and cook over medium-low heat, stirring occasionally, until the garlic is fragrant but not browned, 3 to 4 minutes.

3. Add the cooked spaghetti to the frying pan and toss briefly. Add the parsley, season generously with salt and pepper to taste and toss well.

4 SERVINGS

SPINACH TORTELLINI WITH CREAMY WALNUT SAUCE

9 ounces fresh spinach tortellini with cheese filling
3 tablespoons olive oil
2/3 cup walnut pieces
1 cup heavy cream
1 cup freshly grated Parmesan cheese
Salt and freshly ground pepper

1. Cook the pasta in a large pot of boiling, salted water until tender but still firm, 6 to 7 minutes. Drain well.

2. While the pasta is cooking, heat the olive oil in a large frying pan. Add the walnuts and cook over medium heat, stirring, until the nuts are toasted, about 3 minutes.

3. Add the cream to the pan and bring to a boil over medium-high heat. Cook 1 minute. Stir in the Parmesan cheese. Season the sauce to taste with salt and pepper.

4. Drain the pasta and add to the sauce. Toss gently and serve immediately.

3 TO 4 SERVINGS

BUCATINI ALL'AMATRICIANA

Bucatini are large, hollow spaghetti noodles, which cook surprisingly quickly. This classic sauce gives them a rosy color and the sweet, sharp flavors of bacon, onion and Romano cheese.

1 pound bucatini
6 ounces Canadian bacon
1 medium onion
1 box (26 ounces) Pomi chopped tomatoes or 1 can
    (28 ounces) "pasta-ready" tomatoes
$1/2$ teaspoon salt
$1/2$ teaspoon black pepper
$3/4$ cup freshly grated Romano cheese

1. Cook the pasta in a large pot of boiling, salted water until tender but still firm, 8 to 10 minutes. Drain well.

2. Meanwhile, cut the Canadian bacon into $1/4$-inch dice. Cut the onion into $1/4$-inch dice. Cook the Canadian bacon and onion together in a large covered frying pan over medium-high heat until the onion is softened and translucent and the bacon is lightly browned, about 4 minutes.

3. Add the tomatoes and their juices to the pan and bring to a boil. Add the salt and pepper. Reduce the heat to medium and simmer for 5 minutes.

4. Add the pasta to the frying pan and toss. Transfer to a large serving bowl and sprinkle on the cheese. Toss well.

4 TO 6 SERVINGS

FETTUCCINE ALLA ROMANA

$1/2$ pound dried fettuccine
3 thin slices prosciutto (about 2 ounces)
1 tablespoon unsalted butter
1 carton (10 ounces) Alfredo sauce
1 cup frozen baby peas, thawed
$1/2$ teaspoon freshly ground pepper

1. Cook the pasta in a large pot of boiling, salted water until tender but still firm, 8 to 9 minutes. Drain well.

2. While the pasta is cooking, cut the prosciutto into slivers $1/4$ inch wide to make $1/3$ cup. Melt the butter in a large frying pan and add the prosciutto. Cook the prosciutto over medium-high heat, stirring constantly, until it softens, about 2 minutes.

3. Stir in the Alfredo sauce and simmer 1 minute. Add the peas and simmer 1 minute to heat through. Season with the pepper.

4. Add the pasta to the sauce in the frying pan. Stir to combine and heat through. Serve immediately.

4 SERVINGS

SPAGHETTI CARBONARA

1 pound spaghetti
1/4 pound bacon
2 eggs, at room temperature
3 tablespoons heavy cream
1 1/2 teaspoons freshly ground pepper
1 teaspoon salt
3/4 cup freshly grated Parmesan cheese

1. Cook the pasta in a large pot of boiling, salted water until tender but still firm, 8 to 9 minutes. Drain well.

2. Meanwhile, slice the bacon crosswise into 1/2-inch pieces. Cook the bacon in a large frying pan over medium-high heat, stirring often, until crispy, 3 to 5 minutes. Transfer the bacon and 1 tablespoon of the fat in the pan to a small bowl and set aside.

3. Whisk together the eggs, cream, pepper and salt.

4. Drain the pasta well and immediately return it to the cooking pot. Add the egg mixture and toss to coat the strands evenly. Sprinkle on the cheese and bacon with its fat and toss well. Serve immediately.

4 TO 6 SERVINGS

MACARONI AND CHEESE

1/2 pound elbow macaroni
2 tablespoons butter
2 tablespoons flour
1 cup milk
1 cup grated sharp Cheddar cheese
1 teaspoon salt
1/4 teaspoon freshly ground pepper

1. Cook the macaroni in a large pot of boiling, salted water until tender but still firm, 7 to 8 minutes. Drain well.

2. Meanwhile, melt the butter in a large frying pan over medium-low heat, 1 to 2 minutes. Stir in the flour and cook, stirring constantly, for 2 minutes.

3. Slowly add the milk, stirring constantly. Increase the heat to medium-high and bring to a boil, stirring constantly.

4. Reduce the heat to low and simmer, stirring occasionally, until the sauce is thick and creamy, 2 to 3 minutes. Add the cheese and stir well to melt it into the sauce. Season with the salt and pepper, add the pasta and stir to coat with the sauce. Serve immediately.

4 SERVINGS

TORTELLINI WITH SAGE BUTTER

9 ounces fresh cheese or herb-cheese tortellini
12 fresh sage leaves
1/4 cup unsalted butter
   Salt and freshly ground pepper
1/4 cup freshly grated Parmesan cheese

1. Cook the tortellini in a large pot of boiling, salted water until tender but still firm, about 7 minutes. Drain well.

2. Meanwhile, cut the sage leaves into small pieces. Cook the butter in a medium frying pan over medium heat until it is lightly browned, 1 to 2 minutes. (Do not let it burn.) Add the sage and cook, stirring constantly, until it turns deep green, about 1 minute.

3. Add the pasta to the pan with the sage butter. Cook, tossing gently, until heated through, about 1 minute. Season to taste with salt and pepper.

4. Turn the tortellini into a serving bowl and sprinkle with the Parmesan cheese. Toss well and serve immediately.

2 SERVINGS

SCAMPI PASTA

3/4 pound dried linguine
3/4 pound raw medium shrimp, shelled and deveined
 5 garlic cloves
 1 lemon
 6 tablespoons unsalted butter
1/2 teaspoon salt
1/4 teaspoon freshly ground pepper

1. Cook the linguine in a large pot of boiling, salted water until tender but still firm, 7 to 9 minutes. Drain well and place on a warm platter.

2. Meanwhile, butterfly the shrimp by cutting down the back to open flat. Do not cut all the way through. Mince the garlic and set aside. Grate the colored zest from half the lemon and juice the lemon. Reserve 2 tablespoons juice. Cut the butter into 4 large chunks.

3. Melt the butter over medium-high heat in a large frying pan. Add the garlic and cook 30 seconds. Add the shrimp and cook, turning, until bright pink, 2 to 3 minutes.

4. Stir in the lemon juice, lemon zest, salt and pepper. Spoon the shrimp and sauce over the pasta. Toss and serve immediately.

3 TO 4 SERVINGS

LINGUINE WITH CLAM SAUCE

½ pound dried linguine
2 cans (6½ ounces each) chopped clams
3 garlic cloves
3 tablespoons olive oil
   Salt and freshly ground pepper
2 tablespoons chopped Italian parsley

1. Cook the linguine in a large pot of boiling, salted water until tender but still firm, about 7 minutes. Drain well and place on a warm platter.

2. Meanwhile, drain the clams, reserving the liquid. Mince the garlic.

3. Heat the olive oil in a large frying pan over medium heat. Add the garlic and cook 1 minute. Add the reserved clam liquid. Increase the heat to medium-high and bring to a boil. Cook until the liquid is reduced and thickened slightly, about 3 minutes.

4. Stir the clams into the sauce in the frying pan and heat through, about 1 minute. Season to taste with salt and pepper. Pour the sauce over the linguine and garnish with parsley. Toss and serve immediately.

3 TO 4 SERVINGS

SPAGHETTINI WITH PARSLEY AND CHEESE

$1/2$ pound spaghettini
 5 large garlic cloves
$1/3$ cup chopped Italian parsley
 3 tablespoons olive oil
$1/4$ cup freshly grated Romano cheese
   Salt and freshly ground pepper

1. Cook the pasta in a large pot of boiling, salted water until tender but still firm, 6 to 8 minutes. Drain well.

2. Meanwhile, finely chop the garlic. Combine the garlic with the parsley on the cutting board and chop them together to mix them well.

3. In a medium frying pan over medium-high heat, warm the olive oil for 1 minute. Add the parsley-garlic mixture, stir well to combine with the oil and remove from the heat.

4. Add the cooked pasta to the pan and toss well to coat with the sauce. Add the cheese and salt and freshly ground pepper to taste and toss well.

4 SERVINGS

SPAGHETTI SARDINIAN STYLE

Oregano is a hardy, pungent herb widely used in Mediterranean and Mexican cooking. Consider keeping a pot of it on your kitchen windowsill, and you'll always be ready for this delicious, spur-of-the-moment supper.

½ pound spaghetti
4 large garlic cloves
1 can (2 ounces) oil-packed anchovies, plus 2 tablespoons of the oil
2 tablespoons chopped fresh oregano or 1 teaspoon dried
¼ cup freshly grated Romano cheese
Salt and freshly ground pepper

1. Cook the pasta in a large pot of boiling, salted water until tender but still firm, 8 to 9 minutes. Drain well.

2. While the pasta is cooking, mince the garlic. Remove 5 anchovy fillets from the can and measure out 2 tablespoons of the oil; reserve the rest for another use.

3. In a large frying pan, cook the anchovies in the anchovy oil over medium heat for 2 minutes, stirring and mashing gently to break them up. Stir in the garlic and cook 1 minute. Remove from the heat, add the oregano and stir well.

4. Add the pasta and toss to coat with the sauce. Add the cheese and salt and pepper to taste. Toss well and serve.

4 SERVINGS

MOSTACCIOLI ALLA PUTTANESCA

This robust-flavored sauce requires only a little chopping and no cooking. It's delicious hot, warm or at room temperature, so try a double recipe and let its flavor enlarge for the next day's pasta salad lunch.

$1/2$ pound mostaccioli or penne
  1 can (2 ounces) oil-packed anchovies, plus 1 tablespoon of
    the oil
  3 tablespoons capers
  1 can ($2^{1/4}$ ounces) ripe olives, drained
  1 can ($14^{1/2}$ ounces) "pasta-ready" tomatoes, drained
$1/4$ teaspoon freshly ground pepper

1. Cook the pasta in a large pot of boiling, salted water until tender but still firm, 8 to 10 minutes. Drain well.

2. Remove 5 anchovy fillets and 1 tablespoon of the oil from the can; reserve the rest for another use. Mince the anchovies. Coarsely chop the capers.

3. In a large serving bowl, combine the anchovies, oil, capers, olives, tomatoes and pepper. Stir to combine well.

4. Add the pasta to the sauce in the serving bowl and toss well.

4 SERVINGS

SINGAPORE-STYLE CURRY NOODLES

Rice noodles are the traditional choice for this Chinese restaurant classic, but cooked angel hair pasta will work as well. Dried rice noodles come in a range of widths, from wire-thin to fat fettuccine-like ribbons. Soaked briefly in hot water, they become soft and pliable.

1/2 pound wire-thin rice noodles
1/2 medium green bell pepper
 2 green onions
 2 tablespoons Indian-style curry paste
1/2 pound cooked bay or small shrimp
    Salt and freshly ground pepper

1. In a large bowl, soak the rice noodles in hot water to cover until limp and bright white, about 5 minutes.

2. Meanwhile, cut the green pepper into thin slices about 2 inches long. Cut the green onions crosswise into thin slices.

3. Drain the noodles. Place them on a cutting board in a long thin log. Cut crosswise into 2-inch lengths.

4. In a large frying pan, heat the curry paste for 1 minute over medium heat. Add the green pepper and green onions and cook 1 minute, stirring occasionally. Add the rice noodles, shrimp, salt and pepper and cook, stirring and tossing often, for 4 to 6 minutes, until the noodles are tender and evenly coated with curry paste.

4 SERVINGS

TORTELLINI IN BRODO

This simple main-course soup is a perfect winter supper. Serve it with steamed broccoli and slices of crusty bread rubbed with extra virgin olive oil and halved garlic cloves.

2 cans (14$\frac{1}{2}$ ounces) vegetable broth
9 ounces fresh tortellini
$\frac{1}{4}$ cup chopped Italian parsley
$\frac{1}{2}$ cup freshly grated Parmesan cheese
    Freshly ground pepper

1. Bring the broth to a boil in a medium saucepan over high heat. Add the tortellini, reduce the heat to medium and cook, stirring occasionally, until tender but still firm, about 7 minutes.

2. Divide the tortellini and broth among 4 individual serving bowls. Sprinkle each serving generously with the parsley, cheese and pepper. Serve at once.

4 SERVINGS

DAN DAN NOODLES

Terrific hot or cold, these Asian-style noodles keep well and travel nicely for picnics or lunch at your desk.

9 ounces fresh angel hair pasta
1 medium hothouse seedless cucumber
1/3 cup salted, dry-roasted peanuts
1/2 cup bottled Thai-style peanut sauce
2 tablespoons sugar
   Salt

1. Cook the pasta in a large pot of boiling, salted water until tender but still firm, about 2 minutes. Drain well.

2. Meanwhile, peel the cucumber and cut it in half lengthwise. Cut crosswise into 1/4-inch slices. Finely chop the peanuts.

3. In a large serving bowl, combine the peanut sauce and the sugar and stir well. Add the pasta, cucumber and salt to taste and toss. Add the peanuts and toss well.

3 TO 4 SERVINGS

KASHA VARNISHKAS

Kasha is crushed kernels of buckwheat, a plant rich in protein and fiber with a nutty aroma and taste. Long a staple in Eastern European kitchens, kasha cooks quickly and pairs nicely with pasta in this traditional homey dish.

1/2 pound bow tie pasta
1 can (14 1/2 ounces) chicken broth
1 medium red onion
3 tablespoons butter
1 cup kasha
    Salt and freshly ground pepper

1. Cook the pasta in a large pot of boiling, salted water until tender but still firm, 8 to 9 minutes. Drain well.

2. Meanwhile, bring the broth to a gentle boil over high heat.

3. Chop the onion. In a large frying pan, combine the butter and onion. Cook over medium-high heat, stirring often, until the butter is melted and the onion is softened, about 3 minutes. Add the kasha and stir to combine with the onion. Add the hot broth, stir and cover. Cook until the kasha is fluffy and tender, about 7 minutes.

4. Remove from the heat and turn into a large serving bowl. Add the pasta and toss. Add salt and pepper and toss well.

6 SERVINGS

SPAGHETTI ALLA CARRETTIERA

Credit for this quintessential tomato and basil sauce goes to the drivers of mule-drawn carts who traditionally shuttled produce from villages into the markets of Rome. Use lush sun-ripened tomatoes when the summer sun blesses your garden or farmers' market.

$1/2$ pound spaghetti
5 large garlic cloves
1 bunch of fresh basil
$1/4$ cup extra virgin olive oil
1 carton (26 ounces) chopped tomatoes, such as Pomi,
   drained, or 1 can (28 ounces) chopped tomatoes, drained
$1/2$ teaspoon salt
$1/4$ teaspoon freshly ground pepper

1. In a large pot of boiling, salted water, cook the pasta until tender but still firm, 7 to 9 minutes. Drain well.

2. Meanwhile, chop the garlic. Remove the basil leaves from their stems. Slice the basil leaves crosswise into long, thin strips.

3. In a large frying pan, combine the garlic and the olive oil. Cook over medium heat, stirring occasionally, until the garlic is fragrant, about $1\frac{1}{2}$ minutes. Add the tomatoes, salt and pepper and increase the heat to medium-high.

4. Cook 5 minutes, stirring occasionally. Remove from the heat, stir in the basil, add the spaghetti, toss well and serve.

4 SERVINGS

LINGUINE PRIMAVERA

Primavera means springtime, so early-season vegetables such as sugarsnap peas, snow peas and young spinach leaves would nicely fill the bill in place of the asparagus or zucchini. Whatever you choose, you'll enjoy a rich and healthful one-dish meal.

½ pound linguine
½ pound fresh asparagus
1 medium zucchini
1 cup chopped red bell pepper
1 cup prepared Alfredo sauce
   Salt and freshly ground pepper

1. Cook the pasta in a large pot of boiling, salted water until tender but still firm, 7 to 9 minutes. Drain well.

2. Meanwhile, cut off and discard the bottom 2 inches of each asparagus spear. Cut the remaining tender stalks crosswise into 2-inch pieces. Cut the zucchini in half lengthwise and then crosswise into ¼-inch slices.

3. Bring 3 tablespoons water to a simmer in a medium saucepan over medium-high heat. Add the vegetables, cover and cook 3 minutes. Stir in the Alfredo sauce, reduce the heat to medium and cook until heated through, 2 to 3 minutes. Season with salt and pepper to taste.

4. In a large serving bowl, combine the pasta with the sauce and vegetables and toss well.

4 SERVINGS

PAGLIA E FIENO

Think of egg-yellow fettuccine entangled on your plate with green ribbons of spinach fettuccine, and you'll understand the translation of this popular dish: straw and hay.

4¹/₂ ounces each fresh egg and spinach fettuccine
  2 tablespoons butter
 ¹/₂ cup cream
 ¹/₃ cup freshly grated Parmesan cheese
 ¹/₄ cup chopped Italian parsley
    Salt and freshly ground pepper

1. Cook the pasta in a large pot of boiling, salted water until tender but still firm, 3 to 4 minutes. Drain well.

2. Meanwhile, combine the butter and cream in a large frying pan over medium heat. Cook 2 minutes, stirring often, until the butter is melted and the cream is bubbly and heated through. Remove from the heat.

3. When the pasta is cooked, add it to the frying pan and toss over low heat, lifting the strands to coat them with the sauce. Add the cheese, parsley, salt and pepper and toss well. Serve immediately.

4 SERVINGS

LINGUINE AL PESTO

Classic pesto calls for 6 ingredients, so this *5 in 10* version forgoes pine nuts, leaving the intense flavors of basil, garlic and freshly grated Parmesan to create their culinary magic.

    1 pound linguine
    3 large garlic cloves
  $1/3$ cup extra virgin olive oil
$1^1/2$ cups loosely packed fresh basil leaves
  $2/3$ cup freshly grated Parmesan cheese
  $1/2$ teaspoon salt
  $1/4$ teaspoon freshly ground pepper

1. Cook the linguine in a large pot of boiling, salted water until tender but still firm, 7 to 9 minutes. Ladle out and reserve $1/3$ cup of the pasta cooking water. Drain the pasta.

2. Meanwhile, coarsely chop the garlic. In a food processor or blender, combine the olive oil, garlic and basil leaves. Process until you have a moist, well-combined paste, stopping several times to scrape down the sides, 1 to 2 minutes. Transfer to a small bowl and stir in the cheese, salt, pepper and reserved pasta water.

3. In a large serving bowl, combine the pesto and the pasta and toss. Adjust seasonings and toss well.

4 TO 6 SERVINGS

SPAGHETTI WITH GARLICKY BREAD CRUMBS

Use ready-made bread crumbs for the utmost speed, but if you have a few spare minutes and a loaf of excellent bread left over, recycle it into a supply for your pantry. Toast bread slices until quite dry, crush or grate them into crumbs and store airtight in a glass jar.

$1/2$ pound spaghetti
 3 large garlic cloves
$1/3$ cup extra virgin olive oil
$1/2$ cup Italian seasoned bread crumbs
$1/4$ cup chopped Italian parsley
$1/2$ teaspoon salt
$1/4$ teaspoon freshly ground pepper

1. Cook the spaghetti in a large pot of boiling, salted water until tender, 8 to 9 minutes. Drain, but leave some water clinging to the pasta.

2. Meanwhile, chop the garlic. In a large frying pan, heat the oil over medium heat. Add the bread crumbs and cook, stirring often, until the crumbs are golden and crisp, 2 to 3 minutes. Transfer to a small bowl, leaving most of the oil in the pan.

3. Add the garlic to the frying pan and cook, stirring often, until fragrant, about 2 minutes. Stir in the parsley, salt and pepper and remove from heat.

4. Add the pasta to the frying pan and toss. Add the bread crumbs and toss well. Adjust seasonings and serve immediately.

4 SERVINGS

5 HEARTY MAIN-COURSE PASTAS

Hearty pasta used to mean spaghetti with meatballs, long-simmering pots of homemade marinara sauce, big pans of lasagne and casseroles of golden-crusted macaroni and cheese. These satisfying, crowd-pleasing dishes got the American love affair with pasta off to a glorious start. Layered and slowly baked pasta favorites suit us when time is no object, but for days when you're cooking with an eye on the clock, here is an assortment of hearty dishes in *5 in 10* style, which will come to your table fast.

Many of your all-time favorite hearty pasta dishes show up in the classics chapter of this book, so check there for express-lane versions of the old standards. Here you'll find Lasagne Toss-Up and Rigatoni Pizzeria, *5 in 10* spins on popular themes. These recipes play with favorite tastes in a quick new context.

Big flavors star here as well. Smoked turkey, chicken, sausage, Gouda cheese and clams all have roles to play, as do richly flavored sardines and anchovies, kielbasa and lamb. Accent your menu with a world of exotic ingredients and tastes in Jamaican Jerk Chicken Fettuccine, Cauliflower-Curry Linguine, Greek Pasta and Thai Rice Noodles with Crabmeat Curry. There's no shortage of familiar flavors either. Turn to Ziti with Tomatoes and Cheese, Shrimp and Mushroom Linguine and Tuna-Tomato Shells when you're in the mood for hearty, homey food the *5 in 10* way.

BOW TIES WITH SPINACH, BACON AND BLUE CHEESE

This rich main-course pasta works nicely as a hearty salad, if you have any left. To revive its robust flavors and take off the chill, warm it gently in the microwave for 30 seconds.

1 pound bow tie pasta
3 strips of bacon
2 ounces blue cheese
2 cups frozen peas
   Salt and freshly ground pepper

1. Cook the pasta in boiling, salted water until tender but still firm, 8 to 9 minutes.

2. While the pasta cooks, dice the bacon and crumble the cheese.

3. In a large skillet, cook the bacon over medium-high heat, stirring often, until crisp. Remove the bacon to a plate. Pour off all but 1 tablespoon of the pan drippings.

4. When the pasta is done, stir the frozen peas into the pasta cooking water, drain well and turn the pasta and peas into a large bowl. Add the bacon, cheese and reserved pan drippings and toss. Add salt and freshly ground pepper to taste, toss to mix well and serve.

4 TO 6 SERVINGS

THAI RICE NOODLES WITH CRABMEAT CURRY

Look for Thai curry paste, canned coconut milk and dry rice noodles in Asian markets and specialty food shops. The noodles are sold in 1-pound packages of translucent, brittle, ivory-colored pasta, which becomes bright white and supple after cooking. This dish is ideal with either $\frac{1}{2}$-inch- or $\frac{1}{4}$-inch-wide rice noodles, but it works with fettuccine or linguine as well.

$\frac{1}{2}$ pound rice noodles
 3 green onions
 1 can (6 ounces) crabmeat
$\frac{3}{4}$ cup unsweetened coconut milk
$\frac{1}{2}$ teaspoon salt
 1 tablespoon Thai curry paste

1. Cook the pasta in a large pot of boiling, salted water until tender and bright white but still firm, 6 to 8 minutes. Drain well.

2. Meanwhile, cut the green onions crosswise into thin slices. Drain the crabmeat.

3. Bring the coconut milk to a gentle boil in a large frying pan over medium-high heat and cook, stirring often, until thickened, 2 to 3 minutes. Add the salt and curry paste, mashing and stirring to dissolve the paste well. Cook 4 minutes, stirring often.

4. Remove the sauce from the heat. Add the crabmeat, green onions and pasta. Toss well and serve.

3 TO 4 SERVINGS

NOODLES WITH KIELBASA, CABBAGE AND CARAWAY SEEDS

1 pound wide egg noodles
1 small cabbage
$1/2$ pound smoked garlic sausage, such as kielbasa
4 tablespoons butter
1 tablespoon caraway seeds
  Salt and freshly ground pepper

1. Cook the noodles in a large pot of boiling, salted water until tender but still firm, 7 to 9 minutes. Drain well.

2. Meanwhile, quarter the cabbage and cut away the tough core. Shred the cabbage. Cut the sausage in half lengthwise. Cut each half crosswise into $1/4$-inch slices. Heat the butter in a large frying pan over medium-high heat until melted and bubbling but not brown, 1 to 2 minutes.

3. Add the sausage and cook 2 minutes, stirring often, until lightly browned. Add the cabbage and cook, stirring often, until softened and bright green, 3 to 4 minutes. Add the caraway seeds and cook 1 minute longer.

4. Toss the cooked noodles with the cabbage mixture. Add salt to taste and season generously with pepper.

4 TO 6 SERVINGS

SALMON-DILL BOW TIES

3/4 pound bow tie pasta
1/2 pound salmon fillet
1/4 cup olive oil
1/3 cup minced fresh dill
3/4 teaspoon salt
1/4 teaspoon freshly ground pepper
3/4 cup dry white wine

1. Cook the pasta in a large pot of boiling, salted water until tender but still firm, 8 to 9 minutes. Drain well.

2. While the pasta is cooking, cut the salmon into 1-inch cubes. In a small bowl, toss the salmon with 1 tablespoon of the olive oil, 1 tablespoon of the dill and the salt and pepper.

3. Heat the remaining 3 tablespoons oil in a large frying pan over medium-high heat. Add the salmon and cook 2 minutes, gently turning once.

4. Add the wine, cover, reduce the heat to medium and cook 3 minutes, or until the salmon is just opaque throughout. Add the remaining dill and cooked bow ties to the sauce and toss well.

4 TO 6 SERVINGS

LENTIL AND SAUSAGE STEW

½ pound dried elbow macaroni
½ pound smoked garlic sausage, such as kielbasa
4 celery ribs
2 tablespoons butter
1 can (19 ounces) lentil soup

1. Cook the pasta in a large pot of boiling, salted water until tender but still firm, 7 to 8 minutes. Drain well.

2. While the pasta is cooking, cut the kielbasa sausage into ½-inch cubes. Cut the celery crosswise into ¼-inch slices.

3. Melt the butter in a large frying pan over medium-high heat. Add the sausage and cook 2 minutes, turning often, until lightly browned. Add the celery and cook 3 to 4 minutes, until bright green and softened.

4. Add the lentil soup, stir well and cook until heated through, about 2 minutes. Add the drained pasta and toss to coat with the sauce. Serve hot in shallow bowls.

4 SERVINGS

CAULIFLOWER-CURRY LINGUINE

1 head of cauliflower
½ pound fresh linguine
4 green onions
3 tablespoons butter
1 tablespoon curry powder
  Salt and freshly ground pepper

1. Cut up enough of the cauliflower to make 4 cups of small florets; reserve the rest for another use. Cook the cauliflower and the pasta in a large pot of boiling, salted water under tender but still firm, about 3 minutes. Ladle out and reserve ½ cup of the cooking water. Drain the cauliflower and pasta and set aside.

2. While the pasta and cauliflower are cooking, cut the green onions crosswise into thin slices. Melt the butter in a large frying pan over medium heat. Reserving 2 tablespoons of sliced green onion tops for garnish, cook the remaining green onions and the curry powder in the butter, stirring often, until softened and fragrant, about 3 minutes.

3. Add the reserved cooking water and cook 1 minute. Add the cooked pasta and cauliflower to the frying pan and toss well. Season generously with salt and pepper.

3 TO 4 SERVINGS

THAI RED CURRY SALMON WITH SNOW PEAS

½ pound dried linguine
½ pound salmon fillet
¼ pound snow peas
 1 can (13½ ounces) unsweetened coconut milk
 1 tablespoon Thai red curry paste
¾ teaspoon salt

1. Cook the linguine in a large pot of boiling, salted water until tender but still firm, 7 to 9 minutes. Drain well.

2. While the pasta is cooking, cut the salmon into 1-inch pieces. Remove the stems and strings from the snow peas.

3. In a large frying pan, bring the coconut milk to a gentle boil over medium-high heat, stirring often. Reduce the heat to medium and add the curry paste and salt, mashing the curry paste and stirring to dissolve it in the coconut milk. Simmer until thickened and well blended, about 4 minutes.

4. Add the salmon and cook 2 minutes, stirring gently to coat with the sauce. The salmon should be opaque. Add the snow peas and cook 1 minute. Add the pasta and toss well.

4 SERVINGS

SHRIMP AND MUSHROOM LINGUINE

$1/2$ pound dried linguine
$1/4$ pound mushrooms
$1/4$ cup olive oil
$1/2$ pound raw shrimp, shelled and deveined
   Salt and freshly ground pepper
$1/4$ cup chopped fresh parsley

1. Cook the pasta in a large pot of boiling, salted water until tender but still firm, 7 to 9 minutes. Drain well.

2. While the pasta is cooking, slice the mushrooms. Heat 2 tablespoons of the olive oil in a large frying pan over medium-high heat. Add the mushrooms and cook, stirring often, until softened and lightly browned, 3 to 4 minutes. Remove to a plate.

3. Add the remaining 2 tablespoons of olive oil to the frying pan. Add the shrimp and cook, turning occasionally, until pink, firm and cooked through, 2 to 3 minutes. Turn off the heat, return the mushrooms to the frying pan and season with salt and pepper to taste.

4. Add the cooked pasta to the frying pan along with the parsley and toss well.

3 TO 4 SERVINGS

SMOKED GOUDA SHELLS WITH WATERCRESS

1/2 pound medium pasta shells
2 bunches of watercress
3 ounces smoked Gouda cheese
1/2 cup chopped red onion
2 tablespoons olive oil
   Salt and freshly ground pepper

1. Cook the pasta in a large pot of boiling, salted water until tender but still firm, 8 to 9 minutes. Drain well.

2. While the pasta is cooking, chop the watercress into 1-inch pieces, discarding the tough stem bottoms. Shred the cheese in a food processor or on the large holes of a box grater.

3. Combine the chopped red onion and the olive oil in a large frying pan. Cook over medium heat, stirring occasionally, until the onion is softened, about 4 minutes. Add the chopped watercress to the frying pan and cook, turning often to wilt the greens slightly and coat them with the oil, about 1 minute.

4. In a large bowl, combine the cooked pasta with the red onion, watercress and pan drippings. Toss well, sprinkle on the shredded cheese and toss again. Season with salt and pepper to taste and serve immediately.

4 SERVINGS

FRISCO BAY SCALLOP FETTUCCINE

9 ounces fresh spinach fettuccine
1 medium onion
2 tablespoons olive oil
1 can (14 to 16 ounces) Italian-style stewed tomatoes
½ pound bay scallops
   Salt and freshly ground pepper

1. Cook the pasta in a large pot of boiling, salted water until tender but still firm, 3 to 4 minutes. Drain well.

2. Meanwhile, chop the onion. Combine the onion and olive oil in a large frying pan over medium-high heat. Cook, stirring often, until the onion is fragrant and shiny, about 3 minutes. Add the tomatoes and their juices and increase the heat to high. Cook 4 minutes, stirring often.

3. Add the scallops to the frying pan and cook, stirring often, until they are white, firm and cooked through, about 3 minutes.

4. In a large bowl, combine the fettuccine with the scallops and sauce, season with salt and pepper to taste and toss well.

4 SERVINGS

LEMON-GARLIC SHRIMP LINGUINE

Fresh asparagus pairs beautifully with this tangy dish. Cook the spears in the pot of boiling, salted water and remove and drain them before you put in the pasta, then dress them with breadcrumbs browned in butter.

9 ounces fresh linguine
4 large garlic cloves
1 lemon
3 tablespoons extra virgin olive oil
½ pound raw medium shrimp, shelled and deveined
   Salt and freshly ground pepper

1. Cook the pasta in a large pot of boiling, salted water until tender but still firm, 2 to 3 minutes. Drain and set aside.

2. Chop the garlic. Grate the colored zest from the lemon and squeeze 2 tablespoons of juice.

3. Heat the oil in a large frying pan over medium heat. Add the garlic and cook, stirring often, until fragrant but not browned, 1 to 2 minutes. Add the shrimp and cook 3 to 4 minutes, turning occasionally, until the shrimp are bright pink, firm and cooked through. Remove from the heat, add the cooked pasta, grated lemon zest, lemon juice and salt and pepper to taste. Toss well and serve.

3 TO 4 SERVINGS

TUNA-TOMATO SHELLS

$\frac{1}{2}$ pound medium pasta shells
1 medium onion
2 medium tomatoes
1 can (6$\frac{1}{2}$ ounces) oil-packed tuna
$\frac{1}{4}$ cup grated Parmesan cheese
   Salt and freshly ground pepper

1. Cook the pasta in a large pot of boiling, salted water until tender but still firm, 8 to 9 minutes. Drain well.

2. Meanwhile, chop the onion. Cut the tomatoes into $\frac{1}{2}$-inch chunks.

3. Drain the oil from the tuna into a large frying pan. Heat the oil and add the onion. Cook over medium-high heat until softened, 2 to 3 minutes. Add the tomatoes and cook, stirring often, until they are softened, about 2 minutes. Remove from the heat and add the tuna, stirring well to break up large chunks.

4. Add the pasta and toss. Add the cheese and season with salt and pepper to taste. Toss well and serve.

4 SERVINGS

MACARONI WITH TOMATOES AND SMOKED TURKEY

Smoked turkey livens up the homey taste of stewed tomatoes and cabbage. This is a one-dish meal for a chilly winter night.

½ pound elbow macaroni
 2 cups chopped cabbage
½ pound smoked turkey
 1 can (14 to 16 ounces) Italian-style stewed tomatoes
   Salt and freshly ground pepper
⅓ cup grated Parmesan cheese

1. Cook the pasta in a large pot of boiling, salted water for 7 minutes. Add the chopped cabbage and cook until the pasta is tender but still firm, 1 to 2 minutes longer. Drain well.

2. While the pasta is cooking, cut the smoked turkey into ½-inch pieces.

3. Heat the tomatoes in a large frying pan over medium heat until bubbling, 2 to 3 minutes. Add the turkey and cook, stirring occasionally, 3 minutes.

4. In a large bowl, combine the cooked pasta and cabbage, the turkey and tomatoes and salt and pepper to taste. Toss well and top with the grated Parmesan cheese.

4 SERVINGS

SEASHELLS WITH ANCHOVIES AND PARMESAN CHEESE

Try this dish even if you're certain anchovies are your least favorite food. It's delicious and quick, and may turn you into an anchovy fan, as it did me.

1/2 pound small pasta shells
1 can (2 ounces) flat anchovy fillets, plus 1 tablespoon of the oil
2 tablespoons butter
1/3 cup freshly grated Parmesan cheese
1/4 cup chopped parsley

1. Cook the pasta in a large pot of boiling, salted water until tender but still firm, 6 to 8 minutes. Drain well.

2. While the pasta is cooking, remove 5 flat anchovy fillets from the can and chop them coarsely.

3. Drain 1 tablespoon of oil from the anchovy can into a large frying pan. Add the butter and cook over medium heat until melted. Add the chopped anchovies and cook, stirring gently, for 1 minute.

4. Add the pasta and toss. Add the cheese and parsley and toss well. Serve immediately.

3 TO 4 SERVINGS

PENNE AND ITALIAN SAUSAGE GRATIN

Use sweet or hot sausage or a combination of both to suit your taste here. To save time, buy the cheese already shredded for you.

10 ounces penne
 1 medium onion
 1 pound Italian sausage
 1 jar (26 ounces) bottled tomato and green pepper pasta sauce
   Salt and freshly ground pepper
 3 cups shredded mozzarella cheese

1. Preheat the broiler. Cook the pasta in a large pot of boiling, salted water until tender but still firm, 8 to 10 minutes. Drain well.

2. Meanwhile, chop the onion. Remove the sausage meat from its casing and crumble into a large frying pan. Add the onion and cook over high heat, stirring often, until the sausage meat is firm and no longer pink in the center and the onion is soft and lightly browned, 3 to 5 minutes. Drain off any excess fat.

3. Reduce the heat to medium. Add the pasta sauce to the pan and season with salt and pepper to taste. Simmer until the sauce is heated through, 1 to 2 minutes.

4. Toss the sauce with the pasta. Spoon into a 15-inch baking dish. Top the pasta with the shredded cheese and broil about 4 inches from the heat until the cheese is melted and bubbly, about 2 minutes. Serve immediately.

4 TO 6 SERVINGS

GNOCCHI WITH PESTO AND PEAS

2 medium boiling potatoes
1 pound frozen potato gnocchi
1 jar (10 ounces) pesto sauce
1 cup frozen peas, thawed
$1/3$ cup grated Parmesan cheese

1. Preheat the broiler. Peel and dice the potatoes.

2. Bring a large pot of salted water and the potatoes to a boil. When the water boils, add the frozen gnocchi and cook, uncovered, until the gnocchi float to the top of the water, about 2 minutes. Drain the gnocchi and potatoes.

3. Gently toss the gnocchi and potatoes with the pesto sauce and peas. Spoon the gnocchi into a 1½-quart shallow flameproof dish and sprinkle with the Parmesan cheese.

4. Broil about 4 inches from the heat for 1 to 2 minutes, until the cheese is lightly browned and bubbly.

4 SERVINGS

GRATIN OF TORTELLONI WITH TOMATOES, CREAM AND GREEN PEAS

18 ounces fresh tortelloni
1½ cups heavy cream
3 cans (14½ ounces each) "pasta-ready" tomatoes
2 cups frozen green peas, thawed
Salt and freshly ground pepper
⅓ cup grated Parmesan cheese

1. Preheat the broiler.

2. Cook the tortelloni in a large pot of boiling, salted water until tender but still firm, 7 to 8 minutes. Drain well.

3. Meanwhile, in a medium saucepan, bring the cream to a boil over medium-high heat. Boil, stirring occasionally, until the cream is reduced by half, 4 to 5 minutes. Add the tomatoes and peas and season with salt and pepper to taste. Heat the sauce through and toss with the tortelloni.

4. Spoon the tortelloni into a 15-inch gratin dish. Sprinkle the Parmesan cheese on top.

5. Broil about 4 inches from the heat until hot and bubbly, about 2 minutes. Serve immediately.

6 TO 8 SERVINGS

MACARONI WITH FOUR CHEESES

That handy little box of macaroni and cheese will never taste the same after you've tried this gourmet version. And it's just as easy, after a quick visit to the imported cheese counter of your local supermarket.

1 pound elbow macaroni
8 ounces cream cheese
1 cup crumbled Gorgonzola cheese (about 4 ounces)
1 cup finely diced fontina cheese
  Salt and freshly ground pepper
1 cup grated Parmesan cheese

1. Preheat the broiler. Cook the macaroni in a large pot of boiling, salted water until tender but still firm, 7 to 8 minutes. Drain well.

2. Meanwhile, cut the cream cheese into 1-inch cubes. Toss the warm pasta with the cream cheese, Gorgonzola and fontina. Season with salt and pepper to taste. Spoon the pasta into a 13-inch gratin dish and sprinkle the Parmesan cheese on top.

3. Broil about 4 inches from the heat until bubbly and lightly browned, 2 to 3 minutes.

4 TO 6 SERVINGS

WINTER SUNSHINE SPAGHETTINI

Try this simple pasta on a cold winter evening when you need a sprightly burst of Italian summer on your table. Zucchini are now available year-round, and sun-dried tomatoes capture summer's lush flavors right from the jar.

1/2 pound spaghettini
1/2 cup oil-packed sun-dried tomatoes, plus 2 tablespoons of the oil
2 small zucchini
1 cup chopped red onion
Salt and freshly ground pepper
1/4 cup grated Romano cheese

1. Cook the pasta in a large pot of boiling, salted water until tender but still firm, 6 to 8 minutes. Drain well.

2. Meanwhile, chop the sun-dried tomatoes. Cut the zucchini in half lengthwise, then cut crosswise into 1/4-inch slices.

3. Heat the sun-dried tomato oil in a large frying pan over medium-high heat. Add the onion and cook 2 minutes, stirring often. Add the zucchini and cook, stirring occasionally, until bright green and softened, about 3 minutes.

4. Toss the pasta and the chopped sun-dried tomatoes with the sauce in the frying pan. Season with salt and pepper to taste, sprinkle with the cheese and toss well.

4 SERVINGS

HAM AND MUSHROOM MACARONI

$1/2$ pound elbow macaroni
$1/4$ pound small button mushrooms
 2 ounces baked ham
 2 tablespoons olive oil
$3/4$ cup tomato sauce
    Salt and freshly ground pepper

1. Cook the pasta in a large pot of boiling, salted water until tender but still firm, 7 to 8 minutes. Drain well.

2. Meanwhile, cut the mushrooms lengthwise into $1/4$-inch-thick slices. Chop the ham into $1/2$-inch pieces.

3. In a large frying pan, heat the olive oil for 1 minute over medium-high heat. Add the mushrooms and cook, stirring occasionally, until softened and lightly browned, about 3 minutes. Add the ham and cook 1 minute. Stir in the tomato sauce. Cook until the sauce is bubbly and heated through, 2 to 3 minutes.

4. In a large serving bowl, combine the pasta and sauce. Season with salt and pepper to taste and toss well.

3 TO 4 SERVINGS

ZITI WITH TOMATOES AND CHEESE

½ pound ziti
1 medium onion
3 tablespoons olive oil
1 can (14½ ounces) "pasta-ready" tomatoes, drained
¼ cup freshly grated Romano cheese
　Salt and freshly ground pepper

1. Cook the pasta in a large pot of boiling, salted water until tender but still firm, 8 to 10 minutes. Drain well.

2. Meanwhile, chop the onion. In a large frying pan, combine the olive oil and the chopped onion. Cook over high heat, stirring often, until the onion is softened, about 3 minutes. Reduce the heat to medium-high and add the drained tomatoes. Cook 5 minutes, stirring occasionally.

3. Add the pasta to the frying pan and toss. Add the cheese; season with salt and generously with pepper. Toss well and serve.

3 TO 4 SERVINGS

JAMAICAN JERK CHICKEN FETTUCCINE

When hot-and-spicy is what you're craving, this is a quick, delicious shortcut. Prepared Jamaican jerk sauce is made with hot chile peppers, ginger, lime juice and a chorus of spices, and it packs a wallop of flavor. Serve with a cool, crisp salad of iceberg lettuce and watercress tossed with a soothing sweet-and-sour dressing.

1/2 pound dried fettuccine
1/2 pound skinless, boneless chicken breast
1/2 cup prepared Jamaican jerk sauce
1/2 cup heavy cream
 1 cup frozen peas
   Salt and freshly ground pepper

1. Cook the pasta in a large pot of boiling, salted water until tender but still firm, 8 to 9 minutes. Drain well.

2. Meanwhile, cut the chicken into 1/2-inch pieces.

3. Heat the Jamaican jerk sauce in a large frying pan over medium heat until bubbly. Add the chicken and cook, stirring often to separate the meat, until the chicken is barely cooked through and coated with the sauce, about 2 minutes. Add the cream and cook 3 minutes, stirring occasionally. Add the peas and cook 2 minutes longer.

4. Add the pasta, season with salt and pepper to taste and toss well.

4 SERVINGS

SPAGHETTI AND ITALIAN SAUSAGE

1/2 pound spaghetti
1/2 pound mild Italian sausage
 1 jar (16 ounces) prepared spaghetti sauce
1/2 cup ricotta cheese
1/4 cup freshly grated Parmesan cheese

1. Cook the spaghetti in a large pot of boiling, salted water until tender but still firm, 8 to 9 minutes. Drain well.

2. Meanwhile, prick the sausage all over, place in a medium saucepan and add enough water to cover. Bring to a boil over medium-high heat and simmer for 5 minutes. Drain, cut into 1-inch-thick pieces and return to the pan.

3. Add the spaghetti sauce and cook over medium heat, stirring occasionally, for 5 minutes.

4. In a large bowl, combine the pasta and sauce and toss well. Divide the pasta among 4 plates. Top each serving with 2 tablespoons ricotta and 1 tablespoon Parmesan cheese. Serve immediately.

4 SERVINGS

SAUSAGE AND PESTO LINGUINE

18 ounces fresh linguine
1½ pounds spicy Italian sausage
1 large red bell pepper
12 ounces button mushrooms
1 container (7 to 10 ounces) pesto sauce
Salt and freshly ground pepper

1. Cook the linguine in a large pot of boiling, salted water until tender but still firm, 2 to 3 minutes. Drain well.

2. Meanwhile, remove the sausage from its casing and break the meat into small pieces. In a large frying pan, cook the sausage over medium-high heat, stirring occasionally, until it is no longer pink in the center, 3 to 4 minutes.

3. While the sausage is cooking, cut the pepper into ¼-inch-thick strips. Slice the mushrooms. Add the pepper and mushrooms to the sausage and continue cooking until the vegetables are tender, about 3 minutes. Stir in the pesto sauce and heat through. Season with salt and pepper to taste.

4. Toss the sauce with the cooked linguine and serve at once.

4 TO 6 SERVINGS

LAMB WITH ORZO AND FRESH MINT

1 cup orzo
1 pound lamb tenderloin or boneless leg of lamb
$3/4$ teaspoon salt
$1/2$ teaspoon freshly ground pepper
6 large shallots
4 tablespoons butter
$1/2$ cup shredded fresh mint leaves

1. Cook the orzo in a large pot of boiling, salted water until tender but still firm, 7 to 8 minutes. Drain well.

2. Meanwhile, cut the lamb into 1-inch cubes and season with $1/4$ teaspoon each of the salt and pepper. Slice the shallots.

3. In a large frying pan, heat 3 tablespoons of butter over medium-high heat until bubbly but not brown. Add the lamb and cook, turning, until brown and crispy outside but still pale pink in the center, about 1 to $1^1/2$ minutes per side. Remove the lamb to a plate, reserving the drippings in the pan.

4. Add the shallots to the frying pan and cook until lightly browned, 2 to 3 minutes. Return the lamb and any accumulated juices to the pan. Add the shredded mint and the remaining 1 tablespoon butter.

5. Season with the remaining salt and pepper, add the cooked orzo and toss over very low heat to heat through.

4 SERVINGS

BEEF STROGANOFF

12 ounces fresh fettuccine
 1 pound beef tenderloin
    Salt and freshly ground pepper
12 ounces button mushrooms
 3 tablespoons butter
 1 cup sour cream

1. Cook the pasta in a large pot of boiling, salted water until tender but still firm, 3 to 4 minutes. Drain well.

2. Meanwhile, slice the tenderloin against the grain into $1/2$-inch-thick strips. Season lightly with salt and pepper. Slice the mushrooms.

3. In a large frying pan, melt the butter over medium-high heat until bubbly but not brown. Add the beef strips and cook, turning, until lightly browned, 1 minute on each side. Remove the meat from the pan and set aside.

4. Add the mushrooms to the frying pan and cook 2 minutes, stirring occasionally. Increase the heat to high and add $1/2$ cup water. Bring to a boil and cook 3 minutes, stirring and scraping up the brown bits from the bottom of the pan.

5. Reduce the heat to medium-low and stir in the sour cream. Heat through but do not boil. Return the beef and any juices to the pan. Season again with salt and pepper to taste. Serve over the warm fettuccine noodles.

4 SERVINGS

GREEK PASTA

1/2 pound spaghetti
1 can (2¹/₄ ounces) sliced ripe olives
5 shallots
³/₄ cup (4 ounces) sun-dried tomatoes packed in oil,
    plus 3 tablespoons of the oil
8 ounces feta cheese
Salt and freshly ground pepper

1. Cook the spaghetti in a large pot of boiling, salted water until tender but still firm, 8 to 9 minutes. Drain well, reserving ¹/₂ cup of the cooking water for the pasta sauce.

2. Meanwhile, drain the olives and chop the shallots. Slice the sun-dried tomatoes into thin strips. Pour 3 tablespoons of the sun-dried tomato oil into a large frying pan. Cook the shallots in the tomato oil over medium-high heat until soft, 1 to 2 minutes. Add the tomatoes to the pan and toss to combine. Remove the pan from the heat.

3. Crumble the feta cheese into the tomato mixture. Add the olives and season with salt and pepper to taste.

4. Add the spaghetti and reserved pasta water to the pan and toss the ingredients together over low heat until the mixture is thoroughly combined and heated through.

3 TO 4 SERVINGS

RIGATONI PIZZERIA

9 ounces rigatoni
1 can (2¼ ounces) sliced ripe olives
1 stick (6 ounces) unsliced pepperoni
1 jar (15 ounces) marinara sauce
¼ teaspoon freshly ground pepper
2 cups shredded mozzarella cheese

1. Preheat the broiler. Cook the rigatoni in a large pot of boiling, salted water until tender but still firm, about 8 minutes. Drain well.

2. Meanwhile, drain the olives. Slice the pepperoni into ½-inch rounds and cut the rounds into quarters. Cook the pepperoni in a large nonstick frying pan over medium heat until it begins to soften, about 2 minutes. Add the olives and toss. Stir in the marinara sauce and simmer over medium-low heat for 2 to 3 minutes, until heated through. Season with the pepper. Stir the rigatoni into the sauce and toss to coat.

3. Spoon the rigatoni mixture into a 13-inch gratin dish and sprinkle the mozzarella cheese on top. Place under the broiler and broil about 3 inches from the heat until the cheese is melted and bubbly, about 2 minutes. Serve immediately.

4 SERVINGS

WAGON WHEELS PRIMAVERA

½ pound wagon wheel pasta
1 medium red bell pepper
2 tablespoons butter
1 pound frozen mixed Italian vegetables
1 container (10 ounces) Alfredo sauce
Salt and freshly ground pepper

1. Cook the pasta in a large pot of boiling, salted water until tender but still firm, 7 to 9 minutes. Drain well.

2. Meanwhile, cut the red pepper into ¼-inch strips. In a large saucepan, melt the butter over medium-high heat. When the butter starts to bubble, add the frozen vegetables and red pepper strips. Toss to coat with the butter. Add 2 tablespoons of water to the pan, cover and cook until the vegetables are tender, 1 to 2 minutes.

3. Add the Alfredo sauce, reduce the heat to medium and cook, stirring constantly, until the sauce is hot, 2 to 3 minutes. Do not let the sauce boil. Season with salt and pepper to taste. Add the drained pasta to the sauce and toss to coat and heat through.

4 SERVINGS

RICE NOODLES WITH SAUTÉED GREENS AND CHILI-GARLIC SAUCE

Fresh rice noodles are sold packaged in many Asian grocery stores. If they aren't easily available, use cooked fresh fettuccine.

 1 pound fresh rice noodles
12 ounces bok choy or spinach
 2 tablespoons peanut oil
 3 tablespoons soy sauce
 2 tablespoons Chinese chili-garlic paste

1. If your fresh rice noodles come uncut in folded sheets, slice them lengthwise into 3/4-inch-thick ribbons. Place the noodles in a colander and rinse under hot water for about 1 minute. Shake to drain and separate the strands. Cut the greens into 1-inch pieces.

2. Set a large wok or frying pan over high heat. Add 1 tablespoon of the oil and swirl to coat the pan. Add the noodles and stir-fry for 1 minute, tossing constantly. Add 1 tablespoon of the soy sauce and stir-fry 30 seconds. Turn the noodles onto a serving platter.

3. Heat the remaining 1 tablespoon oil in the wok. Add the greens, toss to coat with the oil and stir-fry 30 seconds. Add 1 tablespoon of the soy sauce and 2 tablespoons of water. Cover and cook 1 minute.

4. Return the noodles to the wok and toss with the greens and remaining 1 tablespoon soy sauce. Add the chili-garlic paste and toss again. Transfer to the platter and serve immediately.

4 TO 6 SERVINGS

BOW TIES WITH KIELBASA

1 pound bow tie pasta
1 kielbasa sausage (about 1 to 1½ pounds)
1 medium green bell pepper
1 medium onion
1 jar (15 ounces) marinara sauce
    Salt and freshly ground pepper

1. Cook the pasta in a large pot of boiling, salted water until tender but still firm, 8 to 10 minutes. Drain well.

2. While the pasta is cooking, cut the kielbasa sausage into ¼-inch slices. Slice the green pepper into ¼-inch strips. Chop the onion.

3. In a large frying pan, cook the sausage over medium-high heat, stirring occasionally, until crisp and brown, about 2 minutes. Add the onion and pepper and continue cooking until the vegetables are soft and fragrant, 2 to 3 minutes longer.

4. Stir the marinara sauce into the meat and vegetables. Cover the pan and simmer together 5 minutes for the flavors to mingle. Season with salt and pepper to taste. Toss the pasta with the sauce and serve.

4 TO 6 SERVINGS

FETTUCCINE IN CREAMY SUN-DRIED TOMATO SAUCE WITH FRESH BASIL

$\frac{1}{2}$ pound dried fettuccine
 1 medium onion
 1 cup oil-packed sun-dried tomatoes, plus 2 tablespoons of
   the oil
 1 cup heavy cream
$\frac{1}{2}$ cup fresh basil leaves
   Salt and freshly ground pepper

1. Cook the pasta in a large pot of boiling, salted water until tender but still firm, 8 to 9 minutes. Drain well.

2. Meanwhile, chop the onion. Cut the sun-dried tomatoes into short, thick ribbons. Cut the basil into thin strips.

3. In a large frying pan, combine the sun-dried tomato oil and the onion. Cook over medium-high heat, stirring often, until the onion is tender, 2 to 3 minutes. Add the sun-dried tomatoes and cook 1 minute, stirring often. Add the cream and bring to a gentle boil over medium heat, stirring often. Boil until slightly thickened, 4 minutes. Add the basil and season with salt and pepper to taste.

4. Add the pasta to the frying pan and toss well. Serve immediately.

4 SERVINGS

LASAGNE TOSS-UP

This express-lane version of lasagne highlights its beloved flavors without the labor of love required to prepare the real thing. If you have a little extra cooking time, use lasagne noodles, either whole or broken up before cooking, for their thick, curly appeal.

$1/2$ pound bow tie pasta
 3 medium zucchini
$1^1/4$ cups prepared tomato sauce with mushrooms
 $1/2$ cup ricotta cheese
 1 cup shredded mozzarella cheese
 $1/2$ teaspoon salt
 $1/4$ teaspoon freshly ground pepper

1. Cook the pasta in a large pot of boiling, salted water until tender but still firm, 8 to 9 minutes. Drain well.

2. Meanwhile, cut the zucchini in half lengthwise, and then crosswise into $1/4$-inch-thick pieces. Combine the zucchini and the tomato sauce in a medium saucepan over medium-high heat. Cook, stirring occasionally, until the zucchini is tender and the sauce is heated through, 3 to 4 minutes.

3. In a large serving bowl, combine the ricotta cheese and about $2/3$ of the mozzarella cheese. Add the pasta, pour the sauce on top, add the salt and pepper and toss well. Sprinkle with the remaining mozzarella cheese and serve immediately.

4 TO 6 SERVINGS

Mediterranean Sunlight Shells

Olives, capers and oregano can bring a bit of provençal sunshine into your kitchen on a gray, wintry day. If you don't have fresh oregano, use another fresh herb such as thyme or tarragon, or substitute 1 teaspoon dried oregano and 1 tablespoon of chopped Italian parsley.

$1/2$ pound large pasta shells
2 tablespoons capers
1 can (6 ounces) oil-packed tuna, undrained
1 can ($2^1/4$ ounces) sliced ripe olives, drained
1 tablespoon chopped fresh oregano
Salt and freshly ground pepper

1. Cook the pasta in a large pot of boiling, salted water until tender but still firm, 8 to 10 minutes. Drain well.

2. Meanwhile, chop the capers. In a large serving bowl, combine the capers, tuna with its oil, olives and oregano.

3. Add the pasta and toss. Add salt and pepper to taste and toss well. Serve warm or at room temperature.

4 SERVINGS

HOT PINK AND BLUE BOW TIES

This is my shortcut version of a beautiful, tasty pasta dish I learned from cookbook author James McNair. Canned julienned beets create its extraordinary color, while toasted walnuts and tangy blue cheese give it sharp, rich flavor. You can substitute Roquefort or Gorgonzola for the blue cheese.

1/2 pound bow tie pasta
  1 can (16 ounces) julienne beets, drained
  1 large bunch of watercress
  1 cup coarsely chopped walnuts
  1 cup crumbled blue cheese (about 4 ounces)
  Salt and freshly ground pepper

1. Cook the pasta in a large pot of boiling, salted water until tender but still firm, 8 to 9 minutes. Drain well.

2. Meanwhile, rinse the beets well under cold water, drain and spread out on paper towels to drain well. Cut off and discard the tough bottom 3 or 4 inches of watercress stalks. Chop the leafy tops coarsely and measure out about 1 1/2 cups. Place in a large serving bowl.

3. In a large frying pan, toast the walnuts over medium heat, shaking the pan often, until lightly browned, 3 to 4 minutes. Add to the bowl.

4. Add the pasta to the serving bowl. Sprinkle with the blue cheese and beets and toss. Season with salt and pepper to taste and toss well. Serve warm or at room temperature.

4 TO 6 SERVINGS

Chicken Pasta in Mexican Mole Sauce

The *mole* (pronounced "moe-lay") sauces of Mexico are complex pastes of spices, nuts, garlic and chili peppers in which meats and vegetables are braised. Look for prepared mole sauces in specialty food shops and Latino grocery stores.

$1/2$ pound dried fettuccine
$1/2$ pound skinless, boneless chicken breast
$1/2$ cup prepared mole sauce
$1/2$ cup heavy cream
$1/2$ cup chopped cilantro
    Salt and freshly ground pepper

1. Cook the pasta in a large pot of boiling, salted water until tender but still firm, 8 to 9 minutes. Drain well.

2. Meanwhile, cut the chicken into 1-inch pieces.

3. Heat the *mole* sauce in a large frying pan over medium heat until bubbling, 1 to 2 minutes. Add the chicken and stir to coat with the sauce. Cook, stirring occasionally, 2 minutes. Add the cream and cook, stirring occasionally, 4 minutes.

4. Add the pasta and toss. Add the cilantro, season with salt and pepper to taste and toss well. Serve hot.

4 to 6 servings

ITALIAN FLAG PESTO NOODLES

This hearty pasta salutes the colors of the Italian flag in a delicious way. The green of pesto, the red of tomatoes and the white of pine nuts and Asiago cheese look terrific together and taste great. If you have a few extra minutes, use dried lasagne noodles, whole or broken into large pieces.

1/2 pound wide egg noodles
 3 large plum tomatoes
 2 tablespoons pine nuts
1/2 cup prepared pesto
1/2 cup freshly grated Asiago cheese

1. Cook the pasta in a large pot of boiling, salted water until tender but still firm, 7 to 9 minutes. Ladle off and reserve 1/4 cup of the cooking water. Drain the pasta well.

2. Meanwhile, chop the tomatoes. Toast the pine nuts in a small dry frying pan over medium heat until golden brown, stirring and turning often to avoid burning, about 3 minutes.

3. Place the pesto in a large serving bowl. Add the reserved pasta cooking water and the pasta and toss. Add half the cheese, the tomatoes and pine nuts. Season with salt and pepper to taste and toss well. Sprinkle the remaining cheese on top.

4 SERVINGS

ROCKET-SHIP LINGUINE

Arugula is a dark, leafy green beloved in salads throughout the
Mediterranean. Its sharp flavor contrasts nicely with milder leaf
lettuces, and its sturdiness makes it delectable when briefly sautéed
with garlic. Also called rocket and roquette, it keeps poorly, and a
little tends to cost a lot. Add it to your garden patch or check out
farmers' markets for a steady, inexpensive supply.

```
 9 ounces fresh linguine
 7 large garlic cloves
12 cherry tomatoes
 4 cups arugula, loosely packed
1/4 cup extra virgin olive oil
   Salt and freshly ground pepper
```

1. Cook the pasta in a large pot of boiling, salted water until
tender but still firm, 2 to 3 minutes. Drain well.

2. Meanwhile, chop the garlic. Cut the tomatoes in half crosswise.
Tear the arugula into large pieces.

3. Combine the olive oil and garlic in a large frying pan over
medium heat. Cook, stirring often, until the garlic is fragrant but
not browned, 3 to 4 minutes. Add the arugula and cook, tossing,
about 1 minute. Add the tomatoes and cook, tossing to soften and
coat them with oil, about 1 minute. Remove from the heat.

4. Add the pasta and toss. Season with salt to taste and a generous
amount of freshly ground pepper and toss well.

4 SERVINGS

6 ELEGANT ENTERTAINING PASTAS

Elegant pasta dishes make ideal centerpieces for festive meals. Dressed up with luxurious and flavorful ingredients and presented with flair, elegant pastas are a snap. This is the time to splurge on luscious, unusual items you don't enjoy every day: smoked salmon, prosciutto and caviar, which make a celebration and add sparkle to an otherwise ordinary pasta dish.

For *5 in 10* showstoppers, give your sauces a flavor boost by adding such fortified wines as dry sherry, marsala and port, or aperitifs such as Pernod and even Champagne. Indulge in wild and exotic mushrooms, fresh and dried, when you find them in gourmet food shops. Seek out imported cheeses, such as Roquefort, Gorgonzola, chèvre and the most flavorful aged Parmesan. Enrich some of your sauces with butter, heavy cream and rich Italian mascarpone cheese.

If your budget makes the fanciest ingredients off limits, you can still create a memorable pasta meal. Visit the best produce purveyor or your local farmers' market to get the most for your money: red-ripe tomatoes, fresh asparagus, sweet white corn and sugarsnap peas. Add the final touch of fresh herbs, from basil and tarragon to thyme, rosemary and dill. Their aroma and taste make the difference between dull and divine, and garnishing with sprigs of whole fresh herbs dresses up your plates naturally.

ANGEL HAIR PASTA WITH ARTICHOKES, PISTACHIOS AND GOAT CHEESE

Goat cheese, known as *chèvre* in French, has the smoothness of cream cheese with a rich, sharp bite. Look for it in the specialty cheese section, often coated in herbs or ash and sold in pyramid-shaped packages or rolled into small logs.

    9 ounces fresh angel hair pasta
1 1/2 cups heavy cream
    2 jars (6 ounces each) marinated artichoke hearts, undrained
  1/2 teaspoon salt
  1/4 teaspoon freshly ground pepper
    5 ounces chèvre (goat cheese)
  1/4 cup chopped pistachio nuts

1. Cook the pasta in a large pot of boiling, salted water until tender but still firm, about 2 minutes. Drain and set aside.

2. In a large saucepan, bring the cream to a boil over high heat. Add the artichoke hearts, including their marinade, and season with the salt and freshly ground pepper. Reduce the heat to medium and cook until slightly thickened, 5 to 6 minutes.

3. Toss the drained pasta with the cream sauce. Crumble the goat cheese over the pasta and toss again.

4. Divide the pasta among 4 serving plates and sprinkle 1 tablespoon chopped pistachios over each.

4 SERVINGS

FETTUCCINE WITH ASPARAGUS AND ROMANO CHEESE

Romano cheese is made from sheep's milk. Like its cousin, Parmesan, Romano has a sharp, salty taste and a dry, grainy texture ideal for grating.

> 1 pound asparagus
> 2 tablespoons cold butter
> 9 ounces fresh fettuccine
> 2/3 cup (about 4 ounces) freshly grated Romano cheese
>   Salt and freshly ground pepper

1. Bring a large pot of salted water to a boil. Meanwhile, cut the asparagus into 1½-inch lengths, discarding the tough ends. Cut the butter into ¼-inch pieces.

2. Cook the pasta and asparagus together in the boiling, salted water for 3 to 4 minutes, until the asparagus is a brilliant green and the pasta is tender but still firm. Drain well.

3. In a large bowl, combine the hot pasta and asparagus with the butter and grated cheese. Toss well and season with salt and pepper to taste. Serve at once.

4 SERVINGS

Gratin of Blue Cheese and Tortelloni

9 ounces fresh spinach tortelloni
1 cup heavy cream
1/4 teaspoon salt
1/8 teaspoon freshly ground pepper
1 cup (4 ounces) crumbled blue cheese
1/2 cup coarsely chopped walnuts
1/4 cup grated Romano cheese

1. Preheat the broiler. Cook the tortelloni in a large pot of boiling, salted water until tender but still firm, 7 to 8 minutes. Drain well.

2. Meanwhile, bring the cream to a boil in a medium saucepan and boil over medium heat until thickened, 2 to 3 minutes. Season the cream with the salt and pepper.

3. Toss the tortelloni with the seasoned cream, blue cheese and walnuts. Spoon the pasta into a 13-inch gratin dish and sprinkle the Romano cheese on top.

4. Place the gratin dish under the broiler and broil about 3 inches from the heat until the tortelloni are hot and bubbly and the topping is lightly browned, about 2 minutes.

3 to 4 servings

SPINACH AND POTATO GNOCCHI WITH ROSY ALFREDO SAUCE AND BLACK FOREST HAM

1 pound frozen spinach and potato gnocchi
8 ounces Black Forest ham
1 container (10 ounces) Alfredo sauce
3 tablespoons tomato paste
3 tablespoons minced fresh thyme
  Salt and freshly ground pepper

1. Cook the gnocchi in a large pot of boiling, salted water for about 2 minutes, until the gnocchi float to the top. Remove the gnocchi with a metal strainer and place in a bowl. Cover to keep warm.

2. Meanwhile, dice the ham. In a large saucepan, combine the Alfredo sauce, tomato paste, ham and thyme. Simmer the sauce over medium heat, stirring often, until smooth and hot, 3 to 4 minutes. Season with salt and pepper to taste.

3. Add the gnocchi to the pan and stir to coat with the sauce and heat through. Serve immediately.

3 TO 4 SERVINGS

GRATIN OF PENNE WITH ROQUEFORT AND HERBES DE PROVENCE

Herbes de Provence is a dried mixture of thyme, summer savory, marjoram and lavender. Its unique flavor marries nicely with the intensity of the Roquefort cheese.

1 pound penne
1 package (16 ounces) frozen Italian-style vegetables
1 cup heavy cream
2 teaspoons herbes de Provence
  Salt and freshly ground pepper
2 cups crumbled Roquefort cheese (about 1/2 pound)

1. Preheat the broiler. Cook the pasta in a large pot of boiling, salted water until tender but still firm, 8 to 10 minutes. About 5 minutes into cooking time, add the vegetables to the water and continue cooking until the pasta is done. Drain well.

2. Meanwhile, in a medium saucepan, bring the cream to a boil over high heat. Reduce the heat to medium and add the herbes de Provence. Boil the cream, stirring occasionally, until it thickens, 6 to 8 minutes. Season with salt and freshly ground pepper to taste.

3. Toss the pasta and vegetables with the seasoned cream and the crumbled Roquefort cheese. Spoon into a 15-inch gratin dish and place under the broiler. Broil until bubbly and lightly browned, 1 to 2 minutes.

6 TO 8 SERVINGS

ANGEL HAIR PASTA WITH SMOKED SALMON AND MASCARPONE CHEESE

Mascarpone cheese is the delectable Italian version of cream cheese. Usually used in sweet desserts such as tiramisù, it provides a creamy companion to the smoked salmon in this luxurious pasta.

1/2 pound thinly sliced smoked salmon
9 ounces fresh angel hair pasta
1 cup mascarpone cheese
3 tablespoons chopped fresh dill
1/4 cup salmon caviar

1. With 2 forks, tear the salmon into bite-size slivers.

2. Cook the pasta in a large pot of boiling, salted water until tender but still firm, about 2 minutes. Drain well.

3. Toss the warm, drained pasta with the mascarpone cheese, salmon and dill.

4. Divide the pasta between 2 or 3 plates and garnish with the salmon caviar.

2 TO 3 MAIN-COURSE OR 4 FIRST-COURSE SERVINGS

ANGEL HAIR PASTA WITH SHRIMP, TOMATOES AND BASIL

3 pounds fresh ripe tomatoes
1 cup fresh basil leaves, plus sprigs for garnish
9 ounces fresh angel hair pasta
3 tablespoons olive oil
1 pound medium shrimp, shelled and deveined
$1/2$ teaspoon salt
$1/4$ teaspoon freshly ground pepper

1. Coarsely chop the tomatoes. Cut the basil leaves into shreds. Meanwhile, cook the pasta in a large pot of boiling, salted water until tender but still firm, about 2 minutes. Drain well.

2. In a large frying pan, heat 1 tablespoon of the olive oil over medium-high heat. Season the shrimp with salt and pepper and add to the pan. Cook until the shrimp turn pink and curl, 2 to 3 minutes. With a slotted spoon, remove the shrimp to a plate.

3. Add the remaining 2 tablespoons of oil and the tomatoes to the frying pan and cook over high heat until the tomatoes are softened, about 5 minutes. Season with salt and pepper. If the sauce seems too dry, add 2 to 3 tablespoons of water. Add the shredded basil and cook 1 minute.

4. Add the shrimp and pasta to the frying pan and toss to coat with the sauce and heat through. Divide the pasta and shrimp between 2 or 3 plates and garnish each with a sprig of fresh basil.

2 TO 3 SERVINGS

SPAGHETTINI WITH PROSCIUTTO AND CREAM

 6 ounces prosciutto
 1 pound dried spaghettini
 3 cups heavy cream
 $\frac{1}{2}$ cup chopped Italian parsley
 $\frac{1}{2}$ teaspoon freshly ground pepper
 2 cups grated Asiago cheese

1. Preheat the broiler. Cut the prosciutto into $\frac{1}{2}$-inch ribbons.

2. Cook the pasta in a large pot of boiling, salted water until tender but still firm, 6 to 8 minutes. Drain well.

3. Meanwhile, in a large saucepan, bring the cream to a boil over medium-high heat. Boil the cream gently until it thickens, about 5 minutes. Add the parsley and pepper to the cream.

4. Toss the drained pasta with the cream sauce, prosciutto and 1 cup of the Asiago cheese. Spoon the pasta into a 15-inch gratin dish. Sprinkle with the remaining cheese.

5. Place the gratin dish under the broiler and broil about 2 minutes, until the cheese is bubbly and lightly browned and the dish is hot.

4 TO 6 SERVINGS

EGG NOODLES WITH SMOKED CHICKEN AND WILD MUSHROOMS

A mixture of wild mushrooms, such as Italian cremini, chanterelles, fresh shiitakes, portobellos and delicate oyster mushrooms will give this flavorful pasta added depth.

 1 pound wide egg noodles
12 ounces wild mushrooms
12 ounces smoked chicken
 4 tablespoons butter
 2 cups heavy cream
   Salt and freshly ground pepper

1. Cook the noodles in a large pot of boiling, salted water until tender but still firm, 8 to 10 minutes. Drain well.

2. Meanwhile, wipe the mushrooms with a damp paper towel to remove any dirt. Slice them very thinly. Cut the chicken into thin slices about 2 inches long.

3. Melt the butter in a large flameproof casserole until hot and bubbly but not brown. Add the mushrooms and stir to coat with the butter. Cover and cook over medium-high heat until the mushrooms begin to soften and release their juices, about 3 minutes. Add the cream and boil, uncovered, until the cream begins to thicken, 5 to 7 minutes. Add the smoked chicken and season with salt and pepper to taste.

4. Add the noodles to the pan, toss to coat and heat through and serve.

4 TO 6 SERVINGS

PENNE WITH SUN-DRIED TOMATO AND LEEK SAUCE

8 ounces penne
3 medium leeks
1/2 cup oil-packed sun-dried tomatoes, plus 3 tablespoons of
  the oil
1 cup dry white wine
1 cup heavy cream
Salt and freshly ground pepper

1. Cook the pasta in a large pot of boiling, salted water until tender but still firm, 8 to 10 minutes. Drain well.

2. Meanwhile, trim the leeks so you are using the white part only. Halve the leeks lengthwise and rinse very well to remove any grit. Cut crosswise into thin slices.

3. Heat the 3 tablespoons sun-dried tomato oil in a large frying pan. Add the leeks to the pan and toss to coat with the oil. Cover the pan and cook over medium-high heat for 2 minutes. Uncover the pan, stir the leeks and cook 1 to 2 minutes longer, until they are softened.

4. Add the wine. Increase the heat to high and boil 3 minutes. Reduce the heat to medium-high. Add the cream and sun-dried tomatoes. Boil until the sauce is slightly reduced and thickened, about 4 minutes. Season with salt and pepper to taste. Toss the pasta with the warm sauce and serve immediately.

4 SERVINGS

PORK TENDERLOIN MARSALA WITH EGG NOODLES

    8 ounces egg noodles
    5 tablespoons butter
    4 large shallots
1½ pounds boneless pork loin
       Salt and freshly ground pepper
    1 cup dry marsala

1. Cook the noodles in a large pot of boiling, salted water until tender but still firm, 7 to 9 minutes, stirring occasionally to prevent them from sticking. Drain the noodles well and toss with 1 tablespoon of the butter. Cover to keep warm.

2. Meanwhile, mince the shallots. Trim the pork loin and slice it into ½-inch-thick medallions. Season the meat with salt and pepper. Heat 2 tablespoons butter in a large frying pan over medium-high heat. Add the pork and cook, turning, until lightly browned on the outside and no longer pink within, 1½ to 2 minutes per side. Remove to a serving dish, leaving the drippings in the pan.

3. Melt an additional 1 tablespoon butter in the frying pan. Add the shallots and cook over medium heat, stirring until soft and lightly browned, 2 to 3 minutes.

4. Add the marsala and boil, uncovered, until the sauce is slightly reduced, 1 to 2 minutes. Whisk in the remaining 1 tablespoon butter to thicken the sauce. Return the pork and any juices to the pan and heat through. Serve over the buttered noodles.

4 SERVINGS

GNOCCHI SMOTHERED IN MUSHROOMS

Again, use whatever mushrooms you find available—fresh shiitakes, portobellos, cremini, oyster mushrooms, chanterelles, morels—singly or in combination.

1 pound frozen potato gnocchi
1 pound wild mushrooms
6 tablespoons butter
1 tablespoon chopped fresh thyme
½ cup marsala or port wine

1. Bring a large pot of salted water to a boil. Add the gnocchi and stir gently. When the gnocchi float to the top, after about 2 minutes, scoop them out and place in a bowl. Cover to keep warm.

2. Meanwhile, thinly slice the mushrooms. Melt 3 tablespoons of the butter in a large frying pan over medium-high heat until bubbly but not brown. Add the mushrooms and toss to coat with the butter. Add the chopped fresh thyme. Cook, tossing, until the mushrooms are tender, 4 to 5 minutes. Add the marsala and boil, stirring constantly, until the liquid is reduced by half, about 2 minutes.

3. Whisk the remaining 3 tablespoons butter into the mushrooms and toss the sauce gently with the drained gnocchi.

3 TO 4 SERVINGS

RAVIOLI WITH CREAMY VODKA AND TOMATO SAUCE

18 ounces fresh cheese ravioli
1/2 cup oil-packed sun-dried tomatoes, drained
2 cups heavy cream
1/4 cup vodka
1 1/2 cups bottled spicy red-pepper pasta sauce
Salt and freshly ground pepper

1. Cook the ravioli in a large pot of boiling, salted water until tender but still firm, 5 to 6 minutes. Drain well.

2. Meanwhile, coarsely chop the sun-dried tomatoes and combine with the cream in a large saucepan. Bring the cream to a boil over high heat. Reduce the heat to medium and boil gently until the cream thickens, about 5 minutes. Add the vodka and red-pepper pasta sauce. Cook the sauce 3 to 4 minutes, stirring occasionally, for the flavors to combine. Season with salt and freshly ground pepper to taste.

3. Pour the sauce into a blender or food processor and puree until smooth. Return the sauce to the pan and add the ravioli. Toss the ravioli and sauce together over medium heat to warm through.

4 TO 6 SERVINGS

SPINACH FETTUCCINE ALFREDO WITH CHAMPAGNE-POACHED SALMON

9 ounces fresh spinach fettuccine
1 cup Champagne
1 pound fresh salmon fillet
1 container (10 ounces) Alfredo sauce
1 cup frozen petite peas, thawed
  Salt and freshly ground pepper

1. Cook the pasta in a large pot of boiling, salted water until tender but still firm, 3 to 4 minutes. Drain well.

2. Meanwhile, pour the Champagne into a microwave-safe dish. Cover with microwave-safe plastic wrap and microwave on High for 1 minute. Uncover the dish and lay the salmon fillet, skin side down, in the dish. Cover again and microwave on High for 6 to 7 minutes, until the salmon is just opaque throughout.

3. While the salmon is poaching, combine the Alfredo sauce and the peas in a medium saucepan. Cook over medium-low heat to warm through. Season with salt and pepper to taste.

4. Remove the salmon from its poaching liquid; reserve the liquid. Peel the skin from the salmon and discard. Break the fish into bite-size pieces, discarding any small bones.

5. Strain ¼ cup salmon liquid into Alfredo sauce. Add pasta and half the fish to the sauce and toss to coat and heat through. Divide the pasta between 2 plates. Top with remaining salmon.

3 TO 4 SERVINGS

TAGLIARINI WITH SHRIMP AND PESTO SAUCE

If tagliarini is not on your supermarket shelf, try this with spaghettini.

  1 pound dried tagliarini
$1/4$ cup pine nuts
  1 pound fresh shrimp, shelled and deveined
  1 container (7 ounces) pesto sauce
  2 cans ($14^{1}/_{2}$ ounces each) "pasta-ready" tomatoes
    Salt and freshly ground pepper

1. Cook the tagliarini in a large pot of boiling, salted water until tender but still firm, 5 to 6 minutes. Drain well.

2. Meanwhile, put the pine nuts in a small, dry frying pan and toast over medium-high heat, stirring often, until lightly browned, about 3 minutes. Set aside.

3. In a large frying pan, cook the shrimp in $1/4$ cup of the pesto over medium-high heat, turning them occasionally until they turn pink and are firm but not dry, about 3 minutes. Add the remaining pesto and the tomatoes with their juices. Season with salt and pepper.

4. Add the pasta to the sauce and toss to coat and heat through. Sprinkle the toasted pine nuts over the pasta and serve.

4 SERVINGS

TAGLIATELLE WITH FRESH HERBS IN CHAMPAGNE CREAM SAUCE

Any mixture of fresh herbs, including Italian parsley, basil, chives, thyme, tarragon or dill, would be appropriate in this garlic-scented cream sauce. Fettuccine can be used in place of tagliatelle.

$1/2$ pound dried tagliatelle
1 cup Champagne or dry white wine
2 cups heavy cream
2 garlic cloves
1 teaspoon salt
1 cup chopped mixed fresh herbs

1. Cook the pasta in a large pot of boiling, salted water until tender but still firm, 6 to 7 minutes. Drain well.

2. Meanwhile, combine the Champagne and cream in a medium saucepan and bring to a boil over medium-high heat. Reduce the heat to medium and boil gently. Crush the garlic through a press. Add it to the cream sauce, season with the salt and continue cooking until the sauce thickens, 7 to 9 minutes.

3. Add the herbs and drained pasta to the sauce and stir to coat and heat through.

3 TO 4 SERVINGS

VERMICELLI WITH SWORDFISH PICCATA

1/2 pound dried vermicelli
2 swordfish steaks (8 ounces each)
   Salt and freshly ground pepper
1 lemon
7 tablespoons cold butter
3 tablespoons capers

1. Cook the vermicelli in a large pot of boiling, salted water until tender but still firm, 5 to 6 minutes. Drain well.

2. Meanwhile, remove the skin from the swordfish steaks and cut the fish into 1-inch cubes. Season the swordfish with salt and freshly ground pepper. Grate the colored zest from the lemon and squeeze the juice. Set the juice and zest aside.

3. Melt 3 tablespoons of the butter in a large frying pan until hot and bubbly but not brown. Add the fish and cook over medium-high heat, stirring occasionally, until firm and crispy-brown, 2 to 3 minutes.

4. Add the lemon juice and zest to the pan. Stir in the capers. Over low heat, swirl in the remaining 4 tablespoons of cold butter to create a sauce. Season with salt and freshly ground pepper.

5. Toss with the vermicelli and divide between 2 serving plates. Serve immediately.

2 SERVINGS

MONKFISH PROVENÇAL

1 pound fresh linguine
1 small bulb of fennel
1 pound monkfish
¼ cup olive oil
2 cans (14 to 16 ounces) Italian-style stewed tomatoes
   Salt and freshly ground pepper

1. Cook the linguine in a large pot of boiling, salted water until tender but still firm, 2 to 3 minutes. Drain.

2. Meanwhile, trim the fennel bulb and cut crosswise into paper-thin slices.

3. Clean the monkfish and cut into 1-inch pieces. Heat the olive oil in a large flameproof casserole and cook the fennel over medium-high heat until soft, about 2 minutes. Add the stewed tomatoes to the pan, cover and cook for 3 to 4 minutes, stirring the sauce occasionally and breaking up the tomato pieces with a wooden spoon.

4. Reduce the heat to medium and add the monkfish to the tomato sauce. Cover and cook until the fish turns white and becomes firm but not dry, 2 to 3 minutes. Season with salt to taste and generously with freshly ground pepper. Add the pasta to the pan and toss to coat with the sauce and heat through.

4 SERVINGS

PASTA SHELLS WITH ASPARAGUS AND BOURSIN CHEESE

1 pound asparagus
10 ounces pasta shells
6 ounces frozen snow peas
8 ounces garlic and herb Boursin cheese
1/2 cup chopped fresh parsley
Salt and freshly ground pepper

1. Cut the asparagus into 1-inch pieces, discarding tough ends.

2. Cook the pasta in a large pot of boiling, salted water for 5 minutes. Add the asparagus and snow peas and cook 3 minutes longer, until the pasta and vegetables are tender but still firm. Drain well.

3. Turn the hot pasta and vegetables into a large serving bowl and stir in the Boursin cheese until it melts and forms a sauce. Stir in the parsley and season with salt and pepper to taste. Serve immediately.

4 TO 6 SERVINGS

RAVIOLI WITH GORGONZOLA AND GOAT CHEESE

18 ounces fresh ravioli
 1 cup heavy cream
 8 ounces Gorgonzola cheese
 8 ounces goat cheese
1/2 cup minced Italian parsley
   Salt and freshly ground pepper

1. Cook the ravioli in a large pot of boiling, salted water until tender but still firm, 5 to 6 minutes. Drain well.

2. Meanwhile, in a medium saucepan, heat the cream over medium-high heat. Crumble the Gorgonzola cheese into a small bowl. Crumble the goat cheese and add it to the Gorgonzola.

3. When the cream is gently bubbling, stir in the cheeses. Cook the sauce, stirring continuously, until the cheese has melted. On a large, deep serving plate, combine the ravioli with the sauce and toss. Add the parsley, season with salt and pepper to taste and toss well.

4 TO 6 SERVINGS

TORTELLONI WITH TOMATO BUTTER SAUCE

This fragrant and buttery sauce has a delicate tomato taste and is very easy to make. Be sure you mince the onion as finely as possible.

```
  18 ounces fresh cheese tortelloni
   1 can (28 ounces) peeled plum tomatoes
1 1/2 cups loosely packed fresh basil
   1 small onion
   4 tablespoons butter
 1/2 teaspoon salt
 1/4 teaspoon freshly ground pepper
```

1. Cook the tortelloni in a large pot of boiling, salted water until tender but still firm, 7 to 8 minutes. Drain well.

2. While the pasta is cooking, puree the tomatoes in a blender or food processor until smooth. Shred enough of the basil leaves to yield 1 cup. Finely mince the onion.

3. In a large frying pan, melt 3 tablespoons of the butter over medium-high heat until bubbly but not brown. Add the onion and cook until translucent and lightly browned, 2 to 3 minutes.

4. Add the tomatoes to the pan and bring to a boil. Reduce the heat to medium-high, cover and cook for 6 minutes. Season with the salt and pepper. Stir the remaining tablespoon of butter and the shredded basil into the sauce. Toss the sauce with the cooked tortelloni.

6 TO 8 FIRST-COURSE SERVINGS

FETTUCCINE WITH BROCCOLI AND BLACK FOREST HAM

To save time here, buy the broccoli florets already cut up. You will find them at the supermarket salad bar or produce section.

1/2 pound dried fettuccine
10 ounces fresh broccoli florets (about 5 cups)
1/2 pound thinly sliced Black Forest ham
1/2 pound Gruyère cheese
 1 container (10 ounces) four cheese cream sauce
  Salt and freshly ground pepper

1. Cook the fettuccine in a large pot of boiling, salted water about 4 minutes. Add the broccoli and continue to cook, uncovered, for an additional 3 to 4 minutes, until the pasta and broccoli are tender but still firm. Drain well.

2. Meanwhile, cut the ham into thin slivers. Shred the cheese in a food processor or on the large holes of a hand grater.

3. In a large saucepan, heat the four cheese sauce over medium heat. Do not let it boil. Add the shredded Gruyère cheese and stir until it is melted into the sauce. Season with salt and pepper and stir in the ham.

4. Stir the drained pasta and broccoli into the sauce. Toss all the ingredients together over low heat until the pasta is coated with the sauce and heated through.

4 SERVINGS

BOW TIE PASTA WITH SHRIMP AND ASPARAGUS

    1 pound fresh asparagus
   12 ounces bow tie pasta
    2 cups heavy cream
   1/2 cup plus 2 tablespoons dry sherry
    1 pound large cooked shrimp, shelled and deveined
       Salt and freshly ground pepper

1. Cut the asparagus into 1-inch pieces, discarding the tough ends.

2. Cook the pasta in a large pot of boiling, salted water for
6 minutes. Add the asparagus and continue cooking, uncovered,
for 3 to 4 minutes longer, until the asparagus and pasta are tender
but still firm. Drain well.

3. Meanwhile, combine the heavy cream and 1/2 cup of the dry
sherry in a large saucepan over high heat. Bring to a boil, reduce
the heat to medium and let the cream bubble gently for 6 minutes.
Add the shrimp and cook until pink and curled, about 2 minutes
longer.

4. Combine the drained pasta and asparagus in the saucepan with
the cream sauce and the shrimp. Add the additional 2 tablespoons
of sherry and salt and pepper to taste.

5. Toss the pasta and sauce together over low heat until the pasta
and shrimp are coated with the sauce and heated through, about
2 minutes.

4 TO 6 SERVINGS

WHISKEY PEPPER STEAKS WITH EGG NOODLES

$1/2$ pound wide egg noodles
 3 tablespoons butter
 4 teaspoons cracked black pepper
 2 New York strip steaks, cut $1/2$ inch thick
   (about 8 ounces each)
   Salt
$1/2$ cup whiskey
$1/2$ cup heavy cream

1. Cook the noodles in a large pot of boiling, salted water until tender but still firm, 7 to 9 minutes. Drain well and toss with 1 tablespoon of the butter. Cover to keep warm.

2. Meanwhile, cut the steaks in half crosswise and press $1/2$ teaspoon of cracked black pepper onto each side of each steak. Heat the remaining 2 tablespoons of butter over medium-high heat in a large frying pan. When the butter is hot and bubbly, add the steaks and cook 2 to 3 minutes on each side, until rare. Remove to a serving plate and season with salt to taste. Cover to keep warm.

3. Add the whiskey to the drippings in the pan, increase the heat to high and boil 1 minute. Add the cream and boil, stirring occasionally, until the sauce is thickened, about 2 minutes.

4. Return the steaks and any accumulated juices to the pan. Spoon the sauce over the steaks and heat through 1 minute. Divide the noodles among 4 serving plates and top with the steak and sauce.

4 SERVINGS

ROCK LOBSTER PASTA WITH TARRAGON

Look for rock lobster tails, usually sold frozen, in your supermarket's seafood section. The buttery tomato and herb sauce is a perfect complement to their sweet meat.

1 pound dried angel hair pasta
3 pounds ripe tomatoes
1 pound rock lobster tails
6 tablespoons butter
$\frac{1}{2}$ teaspoon salt
$\frac{1}{4}$ teaspoon freshly ground pepper
$\frac{1}{3}$ cup chopped fresh tarragon, plus 4 sprigs for garnish

1. Cook the pasta in a large pot of boiling, salted water until tender but still firm, 4 to 6 minutes. Drain well.

2. Meanwhile, coarsely chop the tomatoes. Shell the lobster tails and cut the meat into 1-inch chunks.

3. Heat 3 tablespoons of the butter in a large frying pan over medium-high heat. Add the tomatoes and cook, stirring occasionally, until softened, about 5 minutes. Add the lobster, cover and cook 3 minutes, or until the lobster is pink and firm. Add salt and season generously with pepper.

4. Add the chopped tarragon and the remaining 3 tablespoons butter. Stir until the butter melts and combines with the sauce. Add the pasta to the pan and toss well. Divide the pasta and lobster among 4 serving plates and garnish each with a sprig of tarragon.

4 SERVINGS

THREE-ALARM CHILI CRAB WITH ANGEL HAIR PASTA

Fresh crab is a perfect choice, but fresh cooked lobster, shrimp, scallops or a combination would work well. Look for black bean-garlic sauce and chili-garlic sauce in the international section of the supermarket or in Asian grocery stores. Delicious for an elegant luncheon, this is lovely served on a bed of butter lettuce.

3/4 pound dried angel hair pasta
3/4 cup mayonnaise
1 1/2 to 2 tablespoons bottled black bean-garlic sauce
6 tablespoons bottled chili-garlic sauce
12 ounces fresh lump crabmeat

1. Cook the pasta in a large pot of boiling, salted water until tender but still firm, 4 to 6 minutes. Drain well.

2. Meanwhile, in a large bowl, combine the mayonnaise, black bean-garlic sauce and chili-garlic sauce and stir well. Pick over the crab to remove any shell or cartilage.

3. Reserving 1/2 cup for garnish, toss the sauce with the pasta. Divide the pasta among 4 serving plates and sprinkle the crab over each serving. Drizzle the remaining 1/2 cup of sauce over the crab. Serve at once.

4 SERVINGS

SHRIMP AND PASTA SHELLS IN BLACK BEAN CREAM SAUCE

Black bean-garlic sauce is a powerhouse condiment awaiting you among the glass jars of pungent sauces in Asian markets and in the international section of many supermarkets. In Chinese kitchens, this seasoning paste of salty fermented soybeans is a classic match for fish and seafood. Bay scallops, squid, clams, chunks of sea bass or a mixture of seafood would also work well in this recipe.

$1/2$ pound medium pasta shells
 4 green onions
 1 tablespoon bottled black bean-garlic sauce
$3/4$ cup heavy cream
$1/2$ pound large shrimp, shelled and deveined

1. Cook the pasta in a large pot of boiling, salted water until tender but still firm, 7 to 9 minutes. Drain well.

2. Meanwhile, chop the green onions. In a large frying pan, combine the black bean-garlic sauce and cream and bring to a gentle boil over high heat. Cook 1 minute. Reduce the heat to medium and stir in the shrimp. Cook, stirring often, until the sauce thickens somewhat and the shrimp are pink and curled, 2 to 3 minutes.

3. Add the pasta and toss. Add the green onions and toss well.

3 TO 4 SERVINGS

7 Side Dish Pastas

In a rice-or-baked-potato rut? Let these uncomplicated pastas rescue you from the dinner-plate doldrums. Rice and potatoes usually call for butter, but these simple dishes rely on a rainbow of robust ingredients for color and flavor appeal. Paired with grilled chicken, sautéed seafood, poached salmon or a bamboo steamer of garden-fresh vegetables, these pastas can round out an express-lane meal.

Many side dishes make use of smaller pasta shapes, including small shells, orzo (shaped like grains of rice), tubetti (tiny tubes sometimes called salad macaroni) and couscous, an essential in Middle Eastern kitchens and surely the tiniest pasta on earth. You'll also find bow ties, ziti and egg noodles, seasoned mildly as befits the supporting roles these dishes play.

Once you've tried a few *5 in 10* sides, you'll soon be creating your own combinations. Adorn your pasta side dish with whatever you can glean from the vegetable crisper and the roundup of sauces on your refrigerator door. Pesto, sprightly salsas, Indian-style curry paste and olive oil with balsamic vinegar harmonize beautifully with cucumbers, fresh or roasted sweet peppers, olives, nuts and cheese. If you follow a vegetarian diet or are simply eating less meat these days, you may decide to move Johnny C's Cabbage and Onion Bow Ties, Ziti with Zucchini and Romano Cheese or Curry-Curry Couscous from the sidelines to the center of your dinner plate.

JOHNNY C'S CABBAGE AND ONION BOW TIES

$^1/_2$ pound bow tie pasta
 1 small cabbage
 1 medium onion
 4 tablespoons butter
 3 tablespoons chopped fresh Italian parsley
    Salt and freshly ground pepper

1. Cook the pasta in a large pot of boiling, salted water until tender but still firm, 8 to 10 minutes. Drain well.

2. While the pasta is cooking, quarter the cabbage lengthwise and remove and discard its tough core. Cut the cabbage crosswise into 1-inch strips to make 5 cups; reserve the rest for another use. Chop the onion.

3. Heat the butter in a large frying pan over medium-high heat until melted and bubbly but not brown. Add the onion and cook, stirring often, until softened, 2 to 3 minutes. Add the cabbage and cook, stirring often, until bright green and softened, 3 to 4 minutes.

4. Toss the pasta with the cabbage and onion mixture and the parsley, adding salt to taste and seasoning generously with freshly ground pepper.

4 TO 6 SERVINGS

ORZO WITH PESTO AND PEAS

1 cup orzo
1 cup frozen peas
2 tablespoons prepared pesto sauce
 Salt and freshly ground pepper

1. Cook the pasta in a large pot of boiling, salted water for 6 to 8 minutes. Add the peas and cook until the pasta is tender but still firm, 1 to 2 minutes longer. Drain well.

2. In a large bowl, toss the pasta and peas with the pesto and season with salt and pepper to taste.

4 TO 6 SERVINGS

TUBETTI WITH CILANTRO AND SALSA

1½ cups tubetti
  2 tablespoons olive oil
 ½ cup tomato salsa
  2 tablespoons chopped cilantro

1. Cook the pasta in a large pot of boiling, salted water until tender but still firm, 7 to 9 minutes. Drain well.

2. In a large bowl, combine the pasta with the olive oil, salsa and cilantro and toss well.

4 SERVINGS

EGG NOODLES WITH GARLIC AND FRESH HERBS

This pleasing pasta puts to delicious use any odds and ends of fresh herbs that may be lurking in the crisper drawer of your refrigerator. Any combination will work beautifully, so pick any three or four from this list: dill, tarragon, basil, sage, oregano, rosemary, Italian parsley or thyme.

1/2 pound egg noodles
4 large garlic cloves
1 1/2 cups loosely packed fresh herbs
2 tablespoons extra virgin olive oil
Salt and freshly ground pepper

1. Cook the pasta in a large pot of boiling, salted water until tender but still firm, 7 to 9 minutes. Drain well.

2. Meanwhile, chop the garlic. Mince the herbs. You will have about 1 cup minced herbs.

3. Combine the olive oil and garlic in a large frying pan. Cook over medium heat, stirring occasionally, until the garlic is fragrant but not browned, 2 to 3 minutes. Remove from the heat and stir in the minced herbs.

4. Add the cooked noodles to the frying pan and toss. Season with salt and pepper to taste and toss well.

4 SERVINGS

ZITI WITH ZUCCHINI AND ROMANO CHEESE

$1/2$ pound ziti
3 small zucchini
1 tablespoon butter
$1/3$ cup grated Romano cheese
    Salt and freshly ground pepper

1. Cook the pasta in a large pot of boiling, salted water until tender but still firm, 8 to 10 minutes. Drain well.

2. Meanwhile, chop the zucchini. Melt the butter in a medium frying pan over medium heat. Add the zucchini and cook, stirring occasionally, until it is bright green and softened, 2 to 3 minutes.

3. Turn the pasta into a large bowl. Add the zucchini and melted butter and toss. Add the cheese. Season with salt and pepper to taste and toss well.

4 SERVINGS

PEANUT SHELLS

Crunchy peanuts and the lush flavor and texture of sun-dried tomatoes light up this spunky little dish. Pair it with grilled seafood and spinach sautéed with black pepper and garlic.

1 cup small pasta shells
2 green onions
1/2 cup oil-packed sun-dried tomatoes, plus 1 tablespoon of the oil
1/2 cup dry-roasted salted peanuts
3 tablespoons chopped cilantro
Salt and freshly ground pepper

1. Cook the pasta in a large pot of boiling, salted water until tender but still firm, 7 to 9 minutes. Drain well.

2. Meanwhile, cut the green onions crosswise into very thin slices. Cut the sun-dried tomatoes into long, thin strips.

3. In a large serving bowl, combine the pasta with the green onions, sun-dried tomato strips and 1 tablespoon of oil from the tomatoes. Add the peanuts and cilantro and toss. Season with salt and pepper to taste. Serve warm or at room temperature.

4 TO 6 SERVINGS

CURRY-CURRY COUSCOUS

1 cup couscous
   Salt
3 fresh plum tomatoes
1 tablespoon Indian-style curry paste
½ cup cashews
2 tablespoons chopped cilantro
   Freshly ground pepper

1. In a covered medium saucepan, bring 1 cup of water to a rolling boil over high heat. Add the couscous and ½ teaspoon salt, stir well and remove from the heat. Cover and let stand at least 5 minutes.

2. Meanwhile, chop the tomatoes.

3. Fluff the cooked couscous with a fork. Add the tomatoes and curry paste and toss. Add the cashews, cilantro and additional salt and pepper to taste and toss well.

4 TO 6 SERVINGS

EGG NOODLES IN BALSAMIC VINAIGRETTE

Balsamic vinegar gives a deep, sweet tang to the classic pairing of tomatoes and fresh basil. If your cherry tomatoes are large, quarter them lengthwise.

1/2 pound wide egg noodles
12 cherry tomatoes
 1 cup loosely packed fresh basil leaves
 2 tablespoons extra virgin olive oil
 3 tablespoons balsamic vinegar
1/2 teaspoon salt
1/4 teaspoon freshly ground pepper

1. Cook the pasta in a large pot of boiling, salted water until tender but still firm, 7 to 9 minutes. Drain well.

2. Meanwhile, cut the cherry tomatoes in half. Shred the basil into long, thin strips.

3. In a large serving bowl, combine the olive oil, vinegar, salt and pepper. Stir well using a whisk or a fork. Add the tomatoes and basil and toss.

4. Add the pasta and toss. Season with additional salt and pepper to taste and toss well.

4 TO 6 SERVINGS

PINE NUT PESTO COUSCOUS

Keep a supply of pine nuts on hand to jazz up simple dishes like this one. Toasting them calls for your full attention, as they burn in a flash.

  1 cup couscous
 ½ teaspoon salt
  3 fresh plum tomatoes
  2 green onions
  2 tablespoons pine nuts
  3 tablespoons prepared pesto sauce
    Salt and freshly ground pepper

1. In a covered medium saucepan, bring 1 cup of water to a rolling boil over high heat. Add the couscous and ½ teaspoon salt, stir well and remove from the heat. Cover and let stand at least 5 minutes.

2. Meanwhile, chop the tomatoes into small pieces. Cut the green onions crosswise into thin slices. Toast the pine nuts in a small, dry frying pan over medium heat, stirring often, until lightly browned, about 3 minutes.

3. Fluff the couscous with a fork. Add the pesto and toss. Add the tomatoes, green onions and pine nuts. Season with salt and pepper to taste and toss well.

4 TO 6 SERVINGS

MINI BOW TIES WITH FETA CHEESE

Look for tiny bow ties in the kosher food section of your supermarket or in any market specializing in Jewish and Eastern European cuisines. Salt generously to round out the sharp flavor of the feta cheese.

1½ cups miniature egg bow ties
   4 ounces feta cheese
   1 small red onion
   2 tablespoons extra virgin olive oil
¼ cup chopped Italian parsley
¾ teaspoon salt
¼ teaspoon freshly ground pepper

1. Cook the pasta in a large pot of boiling, salted water until tender but still firm, 6 to 8 minutes. Drain well.

2. Meanwhile, crumble the feta cheese. Chop the red onion.

3. In a medium frying pan, heat the olive oil over medium heat for 1 minute. Add the onion and cook, stirring often, until shiny and tender, about 2 minutes. Add the parsley, salt and pepper and remove from the heat.

4. In a large serving bowl, combine the pasta, cheese and the red onion mixture. Toss well.

4 TO 6 SERVINGS

TUBETTI TABBOULEH

Celebrate the sharp, refreshing Middle Eastern flavors of the classic tabbouleh salad, using small tubes of pasta instead of the traditional cracked bulgur wheat.

1 1/2 cups tubetti
  3 fresh plum tomatoes
  3 tablespoons fresh lemon juice
  1/4 cup extra virgin olive oil
    Salt and freshly ground pepper
1 1/2 cups chopped fresh mint

1. Cook the pasta in a large pot of boiling, salted water until tender but still firm, 7 to 9 minutes. Drain and rinse in cold water. Drain well.

2. Meanwhile, chop the tomatoes.

3. In a large serving bowl, combine the lemon juice, olive oil and salt and pepper. Mix well using a whisk or a fork. Add the pasta and toss. Add the tomatoes and mint and toss well. Serve at room temperature.

4 TO 6 SERVINGS

8 LIGHT AND LEAN PASTAS

Is it possible for something as satisfying and luscious as pasta to be light and low in fat? The answer is a resounding "Yes, indeed!" And pasta's neutral taste makes it the perfect canvas for sauces and condiments, which are rich in flavor yet often low in fat.

Lean recipes can explore the globe, borrowing seasoning ideas from around the world. Check ethnic markets and gourmet specialty shops for seasoning sauces that deliver incredible flavor in record time: plum sauce, sweet-and-sour sauce, black bean sauce and hoisin provide an Asian touch, while Jamaican jerk sauce, Mexican *mole* sauce and Thai and Indian-style curry pastes provide exotic sizzling flavors.

To cut fat while preserving flavor, put aromatic ingredients to work in your kitchen: shallots, garlic, leeks and sweet onions. Roasted red peppers, flavored mustards, soy sauce and citrus fruits also help boost taste.

Lower-fat ground turkey and Italian turkey sausages taste terrific in meat-based recipes, and fish and seafood provide protein in lighter form. When you do use fat in small amounts, use highly flavored varieties, like extra virgin olive oil and Asian sesame oil.

Reduced-fat products have multiplied in the marketplace of late, so check your grocer's shelf for low-fat and nonfat versions of mayonnaise, bottled salad dressings, yogurt and sour cream.

FETTUCCINE WITH ROASTED RED PEPPER-ORANGE SAUCE

3/4 pound dried fettuccine
1 jar (12 ounces) roasted red peppers, drained
1 can (14 1/2 ounces) "pasta-ready" tomatoes, undrained
1 orange
5 medium garlic cloves
   Salt and freshly ground pepper

1. Cook the fettuccine in a large pot of boiling, salted water until tender but still firm, 8 to 9 minutes. Drain well.

2. Meanwhile, combine the roasted peppers and tomatoes with their juice in a blender or food processor. Remove the colored zest from the orange using a zester or a vegetable peeler and add it to the peppers and tomatoes. Cut the orange in half crosswise and squeeze its juice into the blender. Crush the garlic through a press into the blender.

3. Puree all the ingredients in the blender until smooth. Transfer to a medium saucepan, cover and bring to a boil over medium-high heat. Reduce the heat to medium and simmer about 8 minutes, until the sauce has thickened slightly and the flavors are combined. Season to taste with salt and freshly ground pepper.

4. Toss the fettuccine with the sauce and serve hot.

4 SERVINGS

WARM PASTA SALAD WITH TOMATOES, GRILLED ZUCCHINI AND ROASTED PEPPERS

3 small zucchini
1 jar (12 ounces) roasted red peppers
1 1/2 cups orzo
1/2 cup bottled low-fat Italian dressing with Parmesan cheese
   Salt and freshly ground pepper
2 large ripe tomatoes

1. Preheat the broiler. Slice the zucchini crosswise into 1/4-inch-thick rounds. Drain the roasted peppers.

2. Cook the orzo in a large pot of boiling, salted water until tender but still firm, 6 to 8 minutes. Drain and transfer to a serving bowl.

3. Meanwhile, cover a broiler pan with foil and place the zucchini slices side by side on the pan. Brush with 2 tablespoons of the Italian dressing and season with salt and pepper to taste. Broil about 4 inches from the heat for 2 to 3 minutes, until the zucchini is golden brown on top.

4. Remove the pan from the oven and carefully turn the zucchini slices over. Brush with another 1 to 2 tablespoons of dressing and broil 2 minutes longer, until golden.

5. Coarsely chop the zucchini, tomatoes and roasted peppers. Add to the orzo. Pour on the remaining salad dressing and toss to mix well. Serve warm or at room temperature.

4 TO 6 SERVINGS

TURKEY AND SPINACH MACARONI BAKE

Fresh spinach is available cleaned and prepacked in the produce section, which makes it especially easy to include in this *5 in 10* pasta. Ground turkey keeps the dish lean and healthy.

10 ounces elbow macaroni
 1 bag (10 ounces) cleaned spinach
 1 pound ground turkey
 1 jar (26 ounces) low-fat tomato and herb pasta sauce
 2 cups grated low-fat Cheddar cheese

1. Preheat the broiler. Cook the macaroni in a large pot of boiling, salted water until tender but still firm, 7 to 8 minutes. Add the spinach to the pasta water about 2 minutes before draining. Drain the pasta and spinach well.

2. Meanwhile, in a large nonstick frying pan, cook the ground turkey over medium-high heat, stirring to break up lumps of the meat, until it is no longer pink, about 4 minutes. Add the pasta sauce and heat through.

3. Combine the macaroni, spinach and turkey sauce. Mix well. Spoon the pasta into a 15-inch casserole dish and sprinkle the cheese on top.

4. Broil about 4 inches from the heat until hot and bubbly, 2 to 3 minutes.

4 TO 6 SERVINGS

MOSTACCIOLI WITH SPINACH AND GARLICKY WHITE BEANS

Packed with fiber and vitamins, this completely nonfat, vegetarian pasta dish is redolent of garlic and brimming with flavor.

1/2 pound dried mostaccioli
 1 bag (10 ounces) fresh, cleaned spinach
 2 cans (14 to 16 ounces each) Italian-style stewed tomatoes
 4 garlic cloves
1/2 teaspoon salt
 1 can (15 1/2 ounces) white cannellini beans
1/2 teaspoon freshly ground pepper

1. Cook the pasta in a large pot of boiling, salted water until tender but still firm, about 10 minutes. About 1 minute before the pasta is done, add the spinach. Drain the pasta and cooked spinach well.

2. Meanwhile, add the tomatoes to a large frying pan, preferably nonstick. Cook over medium-high heat, breaking up the tomato pieces with the back of a spoon, 2 to 3 minutes.

3. Crush the garlic through a press into the tomatoes. Stir in the salt. Reduce the heat to medium and simmer 5 minutes. Drain the cannellini beans and add to the tomato sauce. Season with the freshly ground pepper.

4. Toss the pasta and spinach with the tomato-bean sauce. Serve while hot.

4 TO 6 SERVINGS

LINGUINE WITH SAUTÉED TOMATOES AND ZUCCHINI

With its delicious and fresh-tasting sauce, this pasta is a mouthful of summer flavors. Make sure you use only the ripest, freshest tomatoes, as the flavor of the sauce depends on their quality.

9 ounces fresh linguine
2 garlic cloves
3 small zucchini
2 large tomatoes
2 tablespoons olive oil
  Salt and freshly ground pepper

1. Cook the pasta in a large pot of boiling, salted water until tender but still firm, 2 to 3 minutes. Drain well.

2. Mince the garlic. Cut the zucchini into 1-inch pieces. Coarsely chop the tomatoes.

3. In a large frying pan, heat the olive oil. Add the garlic and cook over medium heat until fragrant but not brown, about 1 minute. Add the zucchini and toss to coat with the oil. Cook for 1 to 2 minutes, until it turns bright green. Add the coarsely chopped tomatoes and continue cooking until the tomatoes soften, 3 to 4 minutes. Season with salt and freshly ground pepper to taste.

4. Add the linguine to the pan. Toss to coat with the sauce and heat through. Serve hot or at room temperature.

3 TO 4 SERVINGS

LINGUINE WITH TOMATO-ARTICHOKE SAUCE

12 ounces dried linguine
 1 large leek
 2 jars (6 ounces each) marinated artichoke hearts
 2 teaspoons dried thyme leaves
 2 cans (14½ ounces each) "pasta-ready" tomatoes
  Salt and freshly ground pepper

1. Cook the linguine in a large pot of boiling, salted water until tender but still firm, 7 to 9 minutes. Drain well.

2. Meanwhile, trim the leek so you are using the white part only. Halve the leek lengthwise and rinse very well to remove any grit. Cut crosswise into thin slices.

3. Drain the marinade from the artichoke hearts into a medium saucepan. Add the leek slices and cook over medium-high heat until they are limp and lightly browned, about 3 minutes. Add the thyme, the tomatoes with their juices and the drained artichoke hearts to the pan. Cover and cook until the flavors are combined, about 6 to 7 minutes. Season with salt and freshly ground pepper to taste.

4. Toss the drained pasta with the sauce and vegetables and serve at once.

4 SERVINGS

FETTUCCINE WITH BUTTERNUT SQUASH PUREE

1 pound dried fettuccine
2 to 3 garlic cloves
1 medium butternut squash
1 tablespoon olive oil
2 cans (14$\frac{1}{2}$ ounces each) "pasta-ready" tomatoes
$\frac{3}{4}$ teaspoon salt
$\frac{1}{4}$ teaspoon freshly ground pepper

1. Cook the fettuccine in a large pot of boiling, salted water until tender but still firm, 7 to 9 minutes. Drain well.

2. Meanwhile, mince the garlic. Cut the squash in half lengthwise and remove the seeds and strings. Place the squash, cut sides down, on a microwave-safe plate and cover with microwave-safe plastic wrap. Microwave on High until tender, 8 to 10 minutes.

3. While the squash is cooking, combine the olive oil and garlic in a large frying pan. Cook over medium-high heat until fragrant but not brown, about 1 minute. Add the tomatoes with their juices to the pan and simmer 2 to 3 minutes.

4. Scoop the squash from its shell and mash with a fork until smooth. Add the squash puree to the tomatoes and stir to combine. Season with the salt and pepper.

5. Puree the sauce in a blender or food processor until smooth. Return the sauce to the pan. Add the drained fettuccine and toss to heat through.

4 TO 6 SERVINGS

COUSCOUS SALAD WITH ORANGES AND CILANTRO

1 cup couscous
½ teaspoon salt
2 navel oranges
1 tablespoon Asian sesame oil
3 green onions, white bulb and 3 inches of green
½ cup chopped cilantro
    Salt and freshly ground pepper

1. In a small saucepan, bring 1 cup of water to a boil over high heat. Stir in the couscous and salt and remove from the heat. Cover and set aside for 5 minutes or more.

2. Meanwhile, using a small, sharp knife, peel 1 of the oranges, removing all the bitter white pith as well. Hold the orange over a small bowl and cut in between the membranes to release the sections. Cut each section in half crosswise. Cut the remaining orange in half and squeeze out the juice into another small bowl. Stir the sesame oil into the orange juice.

3. Slice the green onions. Toss the couscous with the orange segments, sliced green onions, cilantro and orange-sesame dressing. Season with salt and freshly ground pepper to taste. Serve cold or at room temperature.

4 SERVINGS

ANGEL HAIR PASTA MARGHARITA

9 ounces fresh angel hair pasta
3 garlic cloves
1 tablespoon olive oil
1 can (14$\frac{1}{2}$ ounces) "pasta-ready" tomatoes
$\frac{1}{2}$ cup shredded fresh basil leaves

1. Cook the pasta in a large pot of boiling, salted water until tender but still firm, about 2 minutes. Drain well.

2. Chop the garlic. In a large frying pan, heat the olive oil over medium-high heat. Add the garlic and cook until fragrant but not brown, about 1 minute. Add the tomatoes and basil and heat through.

3. Add the pasta to the sauce in the pan and stir to coat and heat through.

2 TO 3 SERVINGS

MEDITERRANEAN LINGUINE

Here the bold colors of ruby red tomatoes and jet black olives team up with the bold flavor of capers in an appealing, satisfying dish. Using fresh linguine with this uncooked sauce means this pleasing dish beats even the *5 in 10* clock.

9 ounces fresh linguine
2 tablespoons capers
3 large plum tomatoes
1 can (2¼ ounces) sliced ripe olives
2 tablespoons extra virgin olive oil
½ teaspoon salt
¼ teaspoon freshly ground pepper

1. Cook the pasta in a large pot of boiling, salted water until tender but still firm, 2 to 3 minutes. Drain well.

2. Meanwhile, coarsely chop the capers and tomatoes. Drain the olives.

3. In a large serving bowl, combine the capers, tomatoes, olives, olive oil, salt and freshly ground pepper. Stir to combine well.

4. Add the pasta and toss well. Serve warm or at room temperature.

3 TO 4 SERVINGS

FAR EAST FETTUCCINE

Look for plum sauce in the international section of your supermarket, or substitute prepared sweet-and-sour sauce for a tangy alternative.

   9 ounces fresh fettuccine
 1/2 pound frozen Oriental vegetable mix
   2 green onions
 1/2 pound cooked bay shrimp
 2/3 cup bottled plum sauce
     Salt

1. Cook the fettuccine and the frozen vegetables together in a large pot of boiling, salted water until the pasta is tender but still firm, 3 to 4 minutes. Drain well.

2. Meanwhile, cut the green onions crosswise into very thin slices.

3. In a large serving bowl, combine the pasta and vegetables, the shrimp, green onions and plum sauce. Toss to mix. Add salt to taste and toss well.

4 SERVINGS

TORTELLINI IN CREAMY TOMATO SAUCE

Evaporated skimmed milk is the key to cutting back on fat without giving up creamy, satisfying sauces. For an even lighter version, use frozen gnocchi or dried ziti instead of cheese-stuffed tortellini.

9 ounces fresh cheese-stuffed spinach tortellini
1 medium onion
2 medium zucchini
1 cup bottled spaghetti sauce with mushrooms
3/4 cup evaporated skimmed milk
   Salt and freshly ground pepper

1. Cook the pasta in a large pot of boiling, salted water until tender but still firm, 6 to 7 minutes. Drain well.

2. Meanwhile, chop the onion. Cut the zucchini in half lengthwise and then crosswise into 1/4-inch-thick slices.

3. In a covered medium saucepan, bring 3 tablespoons of water to a simmer over medium heat. Add the onion and zucchini and cook, covered, until softened, 3 to 4 minutes. Uncover and add the spaghetti sauce and evaporated milk. Increase the heat to medium-high and bring to a gentle boil. Cook 4 minutes, stirring occasionally.

4. In a large serving bowl, toss the pasta with the sauce and salt and pepper to taste. Serve at once.

3 TO 4 SERVINGS

LOW-FAT TUNA AND BEAN SALAD

$^{1}/_{2}$ pound small pasta twists
 4 green onions
 1 can (6$^{1}/_{8}$ ounces) white tuna packed in water
 1 can (8$^{3}/_{4}$ ounces) kidney beans
$^{1}/_{2}$ cup fat-free ranch salad dressing
   Salt and freshly ground pepper

1. Cook the pasta in a large pot of boiling, salted water until tender but still firm, 8 to 10 minutes. Drain and rinse in cold water. Drain again.

2. While the pasta is cooking, cut the green onions crosswise into very thin slices. Drain the tuna and break it up with a fork. Drain the beans.

3. In a medium bowl, combine the pasta, green onions, tuna and kidney beans. Toss to mix. Add the salad dressing and salt and pepper to taste and toss well. Serve cool.

4 TO 6 SERVINGS

SKINNY MACARONI SALAD

1/2 pound salad macaroni
2 celery ribs
1 cup nonfat mayonnaise
2 tablespoons spicy brown mustard
1/4 cup sweet pickle relish
   Salt and freshly ground pepper

1. Cook the macaroni in a large pot of boiling, salted water until tender but still firm, 7 to 9 minutes. Drain and rinse in cold water. Drain again.

2. Meanwhile, chop the celery into 1/4-inch pieces. In a medium bowl, blend together the mayonnaise and mustard.

3. Add the cool, drained macaroni to the mustard mayonnaise. Add the chopped celery and pickle relish and toss to mix well. Season with salt and pepper to taste.

4 TO 6 SERVINGS

LOW-FAT MACARONI AND CHEESE

Here a basic mornay sauce is lightened up and tossed with classic elbow macaroni for a healthy family favorite.

½ pound elbow macaroni
3 tablespoons reduced-calorie margarine
3 tablespoons flour
2 cups nonfat milk
3 cups shredded low-fat Cheddar cheese
Salt and freshly ground pepper

1. Cook the pasta in a large pot of boiling, salted water until tender but still firm, 7 to 8 minutes. Drain well.

2. Meanwhile, in a large saucepan, melt the margarine over medium heat until bubbly but not brown. Add the flour and cook, stirring constantly, 1 to 2 minutes. Whisk in the milk slowly. Continue stirring until the mixture comes to a boil. Boil, stirring continuously, for 1 minute, until the sauce thickens.

3. Reduce the heat to medium-low and add the cheese, stirring until the cheese is melted. Season with salt and pepper to taste. Toss the sauce with the macaroni and serve.

4 TO 6 SERVINGS

MONTEGO BAY SHELLS WITH SMOKED CHICKEN

Unlike plump fresh or frozen potato gnocchi dumplings, these gnocchi are rotund little dried pasta shells that beautifully capture this pungent sauce with its inviting chunks of smoked chicken and green onions. Be sure to cook the yogurt gently, to keep it from curdling.

½ pound dried "gnocchi" or medium shells
4 green onions
½ pound smoked chicken
½ cup Jamaican jerk sauce
1 cup (8 ounces) plain nonfat yogurt
Salt and freshly ground pepper

1. Cook the pasta in a large pot of boiling water until tender but still firm, 7 to 9 minutes. Drain well.

2. Meanwhile, cut the green onions crosswise into ¼-inch slices. Cut the chicken into long, thin strips.

3. In a large frying pan, combine the jerk sauce and the chicken. Cook over medium heat for 3 minutes. Reduce the heat to low and stir in the yogurt. Cook for about 2 minutes, stirring occasionally, to heat through without allowing the sauce to boil. Stir in the green onions and remove from the heat.

4. Add the pasta, season with salt and pepper to taste and toss well. Serve immediately.

4 SERVINGS

INDEX